THE MAN WHO WAS ORTHODOX

THE MAN WHO WAS ORTHODOX

A Selection from the Uncollected Writings

of

G. K. CHESTERTON

Arranged and Introduced

by

A. L. MAYCOCK

LONDON: DENNIS DOBSON

First published in 1963 by Dobson Books Ltd.
80 Kensington Church Street, London W.8

Printed in Great Britain by
Cox and Wyman Ltd., London, Reading, and Fakenham

CONTENTS

ACKNOWLEDGMENTS   11

INTRODUCTION   13

Passages from the Uncollected Writings of G. K. Chesterton.

THE DEBATER. *Daily News*, July 7th, 1906   81
HUMOUR AND GRAVITY. *Black and White*, April 18th, 1903   81
AN ATHEISTIC NIGHTMARE. *Speaker*, Aug. 10th, 1901   83
THE ANATOMY OF THE JOKE. *Hearst's International*, June, 1922   84
PUNCH AND JUDY, I. *Daily News*, Oct. 26th, 1907   86
PUNCH AND JUDY, II. *Illustrated London News*, Oct. 8th, 1921   88
THE SAINT AND THE DRAGON. *Daily News*, July 8th, 1905   89
A UNIVERSAL RELEVANCE. *Daily News*, Dec. 12th, 1903   89
CREEDS AND COBWEBS. *Daily News*, Feb. 13th, 1906   90
A PLEA FOR POPULAR PHILOSOPHY. *Daily News*, June 22nd, 1907   91
RUBBISH. *Daily News*, June 24th, 1911   93
NO SUCH THING. *Illustrated London News*, Jan. 12th, 1907   94
THE PROTECTION OF THE BIBLE. *Daily News*, April 17th, 1909   96
SPIRITUALISM. *Illustrated London News*, March 15th, 1919   98
THE ENGLISHMAN'S RELIGION. *The Bystander*, June 1st, 1904   100
THE ENGLISH WAY. *Daily News*, March 16th, 1905   100
HIGH OR LOW? *Illustrated London News*, July 14th, 1906   101
STRAIGHT THINKING. *Daily News*, Feb. 25th, 1905   103
A MAN OF DISTINCTION. *G. K.'s Weekly*, March 29th, 1930   104
ST. PIUS X. *Illustrated London News*, Aug. 29th, 1914   106
THE BLACK LINES. *Daily News*, Sept. 9th, 1905   107
THE COSMIC STEW-POT. *T. P.'s Weekly*, Christmas, 1910   108
THE SENTINEL. *Speaker*, Oct. 19th, 1901   110
EVERYMAN. *Blackfriars*, Jan., 1923   110
DEATH OF AN ARTIST. *Speaker*, July 9th, 1904   110
POETRY AND BELIEFS. *Daily News*, June 25th, 1904   113
TWO GREAT TORIES. *Daily News*, Aug. 1st, 1903   114
THE FALLACY OF FREEDOM. *Daily News*, Dec. 21st, 1905   118
LIBERTY. *Daily News*, March 18th, 1911   119
THE SERVILE STATE. *Daily News*, July 29th, 1905   119
THE SIN OF PROHIBITION. *True Temperance Quarterly*, May, 1933   119
AUTOMATIC EVIL. *Daily News*, Feb. 19th, 1910   121

CONTENTS

THE TYRANNICAL SCEPTIC. *Black and White*, March 7th, 1903   122

THE SHAPE OF THINGS TO COME. *Daily News*, Feb. 18th, 1905   123

SKY SIGNS. *G. K.'s Weekly*, June 19th, 1926   123

THE MONSTROSITY. *Daily News*, March 11th, 1911   124

POLITICS AND DISCONTENT. *T. P.'s Weekly*, Christmas, 1910   124

AGAINST DIVINE DISCONTENT. *New York American*, Dec. 15th, 1932   126

RELIGION AND REVOLUTION. *New York American*, April 1st, 1933   128

THE EVIL DAY. *Daily News*, June 26th, 1909   129

WHAT WAS RATIONALISM? *New Witness*, March 20th, 1913   131

FROM DICKENS TO GISSING. *G. K.'s Weekly*, Oct. 17th, 1925   132

THE CORNER. *Daily News*, May 14th, 1910   135

CHAOS. *New York Herald Tribune Magazine*, July 5th, 1931   135

THE VENGEANCE OF VICTORIA. *G. K.'s Weekly*, Oct. 15th, 1932   136

PRIVACY. *New Witness*, Oct. 7th, 1921   137

NORTHCLIFFE. *G. K.'s Weekly*, Sept. 17th, 1927   137

THE VISION OF VULGARITY I. *New York American*, July 22nd, 1933   139

THE VISION OF VULGARITY II. *G. K.'s Weekly*, Jan. 1st, 1927   140

THE HUMBLEST ANIMAL. *Daily News*, March 21st, 1906   143

PUTTING THE CLOCK BACK. *Illustrated London News*, July 8th, 1911   143

THE NUMBER YOU FIRST THOUGHT OF. *Illustrated London News*, Feb. 24th, 1912   144

THE LIVING PAST. *Daily News*, Dec. 7th, 1907   145

THE UNCHANGING VISION. *Daily News*, Sept. 15th, 1906   146

THE WHITE HOUSE. *Daily News*, Aug. 24th, 1907   149

THE ICONOCLAST. *Daily News*, April 26th, 1905   150

THE RETURN OF THE ANGELS. *Daily News*, March 14th, 1903   150

THE NECESSITY OF LUXURY. *Open Review*, July, 1906   153

THE CLUB. *Daily News*, April 10th, 1906   154

THE BIG THING AND THE SMALL. *Daily News*, Sept. 19th, 1908   154

'WORKING OUT THE BRUTE.' *Daily News*, Feb. 3rd, 1906   155

ORANGE PEEL AND THE FALL. *Bystander*, May 11th, 1904   156

ORIGINAL SIN. *Daily News*, Sept. 2nd, 1905   156

THE OUTLINE OF THE FALL. *G. K.'s Weekly*, Sept. 25th, 1926   157

NEUROSIS. *Daily News*, Jan. 18th, 1908   158

THE BATTLE. *Speaker*, Sept. 9th, 1905   159

THE DECORATION. *Illustrated London News*, Feb. 10th, 1906   159

SURPRISE. *Black and White*, Feb. 14th, 1903   160

THE PHILOSOPHY OF PUMPKINS. *Daily News*, Sept. 2nd, 1905   160

'IN THE BEGINNING.' *T. P.'s Weekly*, Christmas, 1910   161

THE SAGE. *Daily News*, Sept. 23rd, 1905   162

INTIMATIONS. *New Witness*, June 17th, 1921   164

CONTENTS

THE LITTLE THINGS. *Speaker*, Dec. 15th, 1900   165

'MERE PARADOX.' *Black and White*, Feb. 14th, 1903   166

THE HIPPOPOTAMUS AND THE CROCODILE. *Speaker*, Sept. 9th, 1905   166

CHANGE AND DECAY. *Illustrated London News*, July 10th, 1920   167

THE ENEMIES OF JOY. *G. K.'s Weekly*, Oct. 11th, 1930   167

AUTOBIOGRAPHY. *Blackfriars*, Jan., 1923   170

LIFE AND LIBERTY. *Daily Sketch*, May 14th, 1931   170

THE LESSON. *Daily News*, June 13th, 1903   173

THE TRUE CRITIC. *Speaker*, May 3rd, 1902   173

FAIRY TALES. *World*, Sept. 27th, 1904   174

THE ETHICS OF FAIRYLAND. *Speaker*, Oct. 12th, 1901   174

DIVINE IMMANENCE. *Daily News*, March 24th, 1903   177

A LOCAL HABITATION. *New Witness*, July 15th, 1921   178

SACRAMENT OR MAGIC. *Illustrated London News*, Sept. 22nd, 1906   179

THE CONCRETE AND THE ABSTRACT. *Speaker*, May 31st, 1902   179

THE LIGHT AND THE HEAT. *Speaker*, Nov. 17th, 1900   180

A NOTE ON COMPARATIVE RELIGION. *Blackfriars*, March, 1923   181

ASSIMILATION AND REJECTION. *Daily News*, March 19th, 1910   183

THE WINTER FEAST. *G. K.'s Weekly*, Jan. 2nd, 1936   183

THE THREE GIFTS. *G. K.'s Weekly*, Dec. 12th, 1931   185

THE SPRING IN THE SOUL. *G. K.'s Weekly*, March 26th, 1932   186

THE PERSON OF JESUS CHRIST. *Hibbert Journal*, July, 1909   188

THE DIVINE COMEDY. *Speaker*, Feb. 9th, 1901   190

THE DRAGON. *Debater*, March–April, 1891   191

ACKNOWLEDGMENTS

I wish to express my gratitude to Mr A. N. G. Richards, Librarian of St Paul's School, for allowing me to study manuscript and other Chesterton items in the school library; to the Rev. R. M. Catling, formerly Librarian of Pusey House, Oxford, for information about material in the Bodleian Library; to Mr Michael Curtis, formerly editor, and Mr S. G. Pryor, formerly Librarian, of the *News Chronicle*, for enabling me to work at the *News Chronicle* office on the files of the *Daily News*. I also thank Mr K. W. Robinson and his staff in the Periodicals Room at the University Library, Cambridge, for much kindness and help. Finally, I am specially grateful to Miss Dorothy Collins who has allowed me to use and to borrow freely from her great collection of *Chestertoniana*, and has given me valuable advice, the most generous encouragement, and permission to use the copyright material here assembled.

A.L.M.

INTRODUCTION

I

Gilbert Keith Chesterton must have been one of the most prolific writers that have ever lived. In a literary lifetime of rather more than thirty years he published nearly one hundred books. He wrote contributions or introductions to about two hundred more. Huge numbers of his essays, letters and reviews lie buried in the files of the old *Daily News* and of such periodicals as *The Speaker, The Nation, The New Witness* and *G. K.'s Weekly.* At one time or another he wrote in pretty well all the important monthlies and quarterlies. For thirty-one years, from 1905 till his death in 1936, he contributed a weekly essay to the *Illustrated London News* – more than sixteen hundred of them in all, of which less than a quarter have ever been reprinted. You find his work – and some of it is of his best quality – in long-defunct periodicals like *The Independent Review, The Optimist, Commonwealth, Black and White, The British Review* and *The Bystander.*

By far the greater part of this immense *corpus* of his journalistic work never got into any of his books and was never intended to do so. Much of it is of purely ephemeral purpose and will probably never be read again except by the occasional specialist. Some of it is of poor quality – when he was tired or overdriven, Chesterton could write like an excruciating parody of himself. But, as Robert Lynd said, it was Chesterton's way to chuck his genius about, and for many years we shall be collecting the gold pieces that he scattered with such magnificent recklessness. The recovery of some of these gold pieces and their arrangement in an ordered setting has been the purpose of the present selection from his writings. Nearly all of it, we think, will be new even to those who know his work best. Apart from a few epigrams and short passages that were repeated in different contexts in his books, it consists of material that has never, to our knowledge, appeared in any of his published books – of material that has never been reprinted and is certainly worth reprinting; amongst the passages here brought together there are to be found, as we believe the reader will agree, some jewels of wit and wisdom that are characteristic of Chesterton at his very best. There will be found too, running through the whole, a thread or outline of some of the most significant ideas that he believed and taught all through his life.

There was always in Chesterton an intense, a passionate desire to be understood. He constantly insisted that truth, in whatever form it is apprehended, should be a public possession. If a man has anything of value to say, it is his duty to say it and to go on saying it as clearly and publicly as possible. That is one of Chesterton's essential characteristics as a writer. He taught. He explained. He taught men to see and understand things that they had never seen or understood before. We do not always recognize – it became especially apparent in his latter years when he began broadcasting – that he had all the gifts of the great teacher – lucidity, patience, a never-failing freshness and originality of mind, a total absence of pomposity or self-importance, and, above all, an intense concern with the importance of what he had to say. He never minded repeating himself; in a sense he may be said to have gone on repeating himself all his life. Anyone familiar with his books will recall instances of the same idea cropping up again and again in this place and that, and being driven home with every variety of illustration and emphasis. Finally, he was a master of the two most powerful instruments by which truth can be communicated from one mind to another. These two instruments are paradox and analogy; Chesterton excelled in the use of both.

Throughout his life he wrote ceaselessly and spontaneously, pouring out the riches of an ever-fertile mind on every kind of topic and never wishing to be thought of as anything more than a journalist. He was entirely unconcerned with renown.

'I have no feeling for immortality', he once said. 'I don't care for anything except to be in the present stress of life as it is. I would rather live now and die, from an artistic point of view, than keep aloof and write things that will remain in the world hundreds of years after my death. What I say is subject to some modification.

It so happens that I couldn't be immortal: but if I could, I shouldn't want to be. What I value in my own work is what I may succeed in striking out of others.'*

These words were written when Chesterton was still a young man, and he would certainly have stood by them to the end of his life. He always regarded himself, first and foremost, as a journalist; and it is important to an understanding of his mind to recognize that he did tend to see things with the eyes of a journalist. But it is also important to realize that he was a journalist of a kind that is now extinct. He was never set a task by anybody. He wrote exactly what he wished to write, speaking his mind with absolute freedom on whatever topic he chose to discuss, professing no knowledge beyond that of the ordinary educated man and dealing with events and ideas in the light of his own clearly defined principles. During his lifetime there occurred that immense revolution in the world of journalism of which Alfred Harmsworth was the pioneer – a revolution by which the journalist, from being a careful and responsible reporter of events and an expert and sometimes influential commentator on public affairs, became, as Chesterton himself put it, 'a man who writes things on the backs of advertisements'. Chesterton saw that revolution take place and he saw its full significance – is there any institution in the world, he once asked, that does harm on so gigantic a scale as the press? For himself, of course, he retained his complete independence as a journalist throughout his life; but the point is that, when we speak of him (as he spoke of himself) as a journalist, we must realize that we are using the word in this special sense and speaking of a kind of authorship that has hardly survived to our own time.

Chesterton's entry into the world of journalism dates from the latter part of 1899 when he started writing regularly for *The Speaker*. It introduced him to a whole new world – to the racket and excitement and, as he pictured it, the romance of Fleet Street, the late hours and night life of its taverns, the Bohemian flavour of its noisy comradeship, and its habits of interminable talk and discussion. Fleet Street was still a place where anything could

* *Public Opinion*, September 29th, 1905.

happen, a place where every shade of political opinion was violently canvassed and where judgements could be based on the facts behind the published news, a place of random work and riotous recreation and unfailing comedy, of fierce rivalries and generous friendships and queer associations; a place, in fact, to exhilarate any man with a sense of romance and independence.

In those early days Chesterton's imagination was held by the sheer romance of it all – 'the great lights burning on through darkness to dawn and the roar of the printing wheels weaving the destinies of another day.' The modern newspaper seemed to him the greatest enterprise in anonymity since the Gothic cathedrals. The complex process of its production, its daily appearance on a thousand breakfast-tables, was not only a marvel of skill and organization. It was a great adventure, renewed from day to day in infinite variety.

'Nothing', he wrote, 'looks more neat and regular than a newspaper, with its parallel columns, its mechanical printing, its detailed facts and figures, its responsible, polysyllabic leading articles. Nothing, as a matter of fact, goes every night through more agonies of adventure, more hairbreadth escapes, desperate expedients, crucial councils, random compromises or barely averted catastrophes. Seen from the outside, it seems to come round as automatically as the clock and as silently as the dawn. Seen from the inside, it gives all its organizers a gasp of relief every morning to see that it has come out at all.'*

The air of Fleet Street was indeed a powerful stimulant and Chesterton's huge enjoyment of it all is reflected in the buoyancy and exuberance of all his journalism in those years. He was a real journalist in being able to write anywhere and at any time – in railway stations or in bed or standing under a lamp-post or on top of a bus or half way up the stairs to his flat in Battersea. Many of his articles were written in Fleet Street taverns where, indifferent to noise and disturbance and always ready to be interrupted, he would sit covering page after page with his uniquely decorative handwriting.

'Your friend,' murmured a head waiter to Charles Masterman,

* 'The Real Journalist', in *A Miscellany of Men*, p. 99.

16

'he very clever man. He sit and laugh. And then he write. And then he laugh at what he write.'

His huge figure, as he loomed absent-mindedly across the road whilst a policeman held up the traffic, or decanted himself from a hansom-cab outside the *Daily News* office, was one of the familiar and entertaining landmarks of Edwardian Fleet Street. After he moved out of London to Beaconsfield in 1909, his visits became relatively infrequent; but all his journalistic work was continued without interruption and, it may be added, with real improvement of quality. Of those pre-1914 books of essays, *Tremendous Trifles, All Things Considered, Alarms and Discursions* and *A Miscellany of Men* (all consisting entirely of articles printed in the various papers for which he wrote), it is safe to say that each is better than the previous one. It may also be remarked that, if Chesterton had stayed racketing about in Fleet Street for much longer than he did, his health would certainly have given way; the illness and breakdown from which he nearly died in 1914, would probably have come several years earlier and might well have killed him. The move to Beaconsfield was a beneficial one in every way.

In his Fleet Street days, and indeed until the outbreak of the First World War – Chesterton was a journalist in the same sense that men like Andrew Lang, Clement Shorter, Arthur Quiller-Couch, Wilfred Whitten and Robertson Nicoll were journalists. They belonged to the great tradition and lineage of English men of letters. All of them wrote regularly in various papers. Some did a good deal of reading for different firms of publishers. In the main, their interests were literary and it was as literary critics that much of their best and most influential work was done. Andrew Lang did a weekly essay, usually on a literary or historical theme, in the *Illustrated London News*; Whitten for a good many years wrote the famous 'Letters to Gog and Magog' in *John o' London's*; Nicoll was the tireless editor of the *British Weekly* and a prolific contributor to many journals and reviews; Shorter's literary page in the *Sphere* probably did more than any other feature of its kind to maintain high standards of criticism and to help the ordinary reader both to appreciate the great writers of the past and to enjoy the best contemporary authorship. Such men as these wrote with authority on all sorts of topics and their judgements commanded respect. They were not scholars in the technical sense; but they were very widely read and some of them made themselves acknowledged experts in this or that specialized field of study. J. L. Hammond did important work in the field of English economic history. E. V. Lucas wrote a standard life of Charles Lamb. Belloc made serious contributions to scholarship in his books on the French Revolution.

There were, of course, the academic scholars – George Saintsbury at Edinburgh, W. P. Ker in London, C. H. Herford, Sir Walter Raleigh and others. But it must be remembered that the development of English studies in our universities is a thing of quite recent growth; and if we wished to find the present-day counterparts of those literary journalists of a bygone age, we should probably look for them in the English faculties of the universities, where so much first-class work, both critical and creative, has been done in the past generation. More than one of the Edwardian men of letters did in fact enter the academic world, and it was in just recognition of their talents and learning that they did so. Churton Collins went to Birmingham as professor in 1904; rather later, Arthur Quiller-Couch accepted the Chair of English in Cambridge and held it with distinction for nearly twenty years. And it is interesting to recall that the Birmingham professorship, prior to its acceptance by Collins, was offered to Chesterton, then just past his thirtieth birthday. He had little hesitation in refusing it and he was no doubt right in doing so; but that is not to deny that he could have achieved eminence in the world of scholarship, had he so chosen.

At that time his reputation as one of the most brilliant and original writers of his time was already established. He had published four books – *The Wild Knight, The Defendant, Twelve Types* and the startling essay on *Robert Browning* in the *English Men of Letters* series which had so much annoyed the pedants by its inaccuracies of fact and quotation, but had been recognized at once as one of the most profound interpretations of Browning that had yet been written. Certainly it was a book that no student of Browning could ignore, and that is as true today as it was when the book was first published. One may doubt the correctness of some of its judgements. One may deplore, if one wishes, the many digressions in which the author seems to seize any pretext for going off into his own reflections about anything in heaven or earth. But the digressions are themselves extremely illuminating commentaries upon Browning's thought; and the biographical sections give an astonishingly graphic portrait of the man himself. The book has a power and fascination that cannot easily be defined or exaggerated; and it is safe to say that it is the kind of book that Chesterton always most enjoyed writing.

The *Browning* established him in the front rank of the younger literary critics. It marked the end of his apprenticeship – he said himself that it marked the end of his youth. And it is interesting to consider very briefly the achievement of the ten years that were to ensue – the ten years between the appearance of his next book, the little monograph on Watts, and the illness that struck him down in the autumn of 1914. It was, in a very real sense, the great decade of his life. It is, of course, true that some of his finest work belongs to the later years of the 1920s and 1930s. But, speaking generally, it is true to say that between 1904 and 1914 his creative powers were at their highest. The sheer volume, quite apart from the quality, of what he wrote during those years, is astounding. He wrote his five full-length romances, *The Napoleon of Notting Hill*, *The Man Who was Thursday*, *The Ball and the Cross*, *Manalive* and *The Flying Inn*. He wrote two substantial books on Dickens, the short study of Blake and the Home University volume on *The Victorian Age in Literature* – surely one of his best books. He wrote the first two volumes of the Father Brown stories, his play *Magic*, the critical study of Bernard Shaw, the sociological essay *What's Wrong with the World*, in addition to two of his most famous books, *Heretics* and *Orthodoxy*. There was the delightful *Club of Queer Trades* and the epic *Ballad of the White Horse*, followed by a volume of poems which included some of his best light verse and the memorable *Lepanto*. Finally, he published, during these ten years, four volumes of essays *(Tremendous Trifles, All Things Considered, Alarms and Discursions and A Miscellany of Men)* chosen from his weekly contributions to the

Daily News and the *Illustrated London News*. And all this takes no account of a large number of lectures and addresses delivered to all sorts of gatherings in many different places.

It would be difficult to parallel so enormous an output and, in particular, difficult to rival its versatility. In that strongly individual manner of his, Chesterton played upon almost the whole orchestra of literary expression, using one instrument after another with an exuberant, if somewhat uneven skill. Yet, in all the luxuriant variety of his work, there runs through it a quality that is especially characteristic of his achievement as a whole – a quality of unity and consistency. It would be difficult, even roughly, to date the order of his books as displaying successive phases in the development of his style or even of his thought. Even with his books of essays, whilst it might be argued that the play of wit and fancy of the earlier collections is not sustained in the later ones with their more mature wisdom and their more solemn notes of melancholy and warning, the whole underlying philosophy is clear and consistent throughout; and in the passages brought together in this book it is interesting to see how often a series of paragraphs, written at different times over a period of thirty years, fall into a natural sequence of thought. No one can doubt that Chesterton's reception into the Roman Church affected him to the depths of his soul; he regarded it as by far the most important event of his life. But it remains true – and this is a matter on which more will be said in a moment – that his final conversion came not to destroy, but to fulfil. As his old friend, Professor Emile Cammaerts, put it:

'He moved from one house to the other with all his treasures and belongings, discarding nothing. Every one of his works found again a place on his shelves and not one of them caused him a pang of regret.'

Much of Chesterton's finest journalism, and certainly a high proportion of those gold pieces of which Robert Lynd spoke, are to be found in the files of the old *Daily News*. The reader of the present collection may be surprised at the number of passages taken from this particular source; but it will be agreed, we think, that they are representative of Chesterton's thought at its best.

The essay entitled 'Two Great Tories', to take a single instance, is surely amongst the best that he ever wrote.

It was A. G. Gardiner, as editor of the *Daily News*, who started Chesterton on the series of Saturday articles which were to become one of the most widely read features in contemporary journalism. They appeared usually in the right-hand column of the editorial page and it has been said that the circulation of the paper on Saturdays was often double that of any other day of the week.* Here Chesterton had an absolutely free hand, whereas in his weekly column in the *Illustrated London News* it was, we believe, an unwritten agreement with the paper that he would not write controversially on politics, science or religion – a fact which sufficiently explains the relative dullness and prolixity of a good many of the *Illustrated London News* essays.

But there was always something incongruous and even comical about his position as a *Daily News* man. It is true that, as an enthusiastic young Liberal, he was, at any rate in the early years, sound enough from the political angle. But it is certain that many of his articles, if submitted by anyone else, would have been promptly turned down as being at complete variance with the policy of the paper and the tastes of its readers. The *Daily News,* as a nonconformist organ, took a strong line on the temperance and licensing questions; it was vigorously anti-clerical in religious matters; and its ownership by the Cadbury family was naturally reflected in a definitely pacifist international policy. And week after week Chesterton went on writing about the high romance of military valour and the merry comradeship of the public house and the wisdom of the medieval schoolmen and the stuffy bigotry of the Puritans, and expounded a philosophy of life that was inspired through and through by the majestic truths of Catholic theology. From time to time the correspondence columns bristled with indignant letters of protest and disagreement; and thus, as Chesterton once observed, was discovered the great journalistic maxim that, if you can only make people angry enough, they will write half your paper for you for nothing. But this was all, so to say, part of

* The first of these essays – the signed Saturday article, as distinct from his many contributions to the book page – appeared on February 28th, 1903.

the fun. Chesterton's value to the *Daily News* was sufficiently shown by the circulation figures.

II

We have said that Chesterton was a journalist in the sense that many of the great English men of letters have been journalists. A good many of his weekly essays were of sufficient general interest and permanent value to be collected every year or two and published in book form. That kind of journalism no longer exists. The essay as a literary form has had its day – Chesterton was one of the last of the great English essayists. But he was also a journalist in another forgotten sense of the word. In his early years in Fleet Street, journalism was still, broadly speaking, a profession rather than a trade. The newspapers and reviews were concerned to keep the reading public informed of events and happenings in the country and in the world at large, and to express the views, by way of interpretation and comment, of an individual or group of individuals, each of whom wrote under his own name and thus accepted personal responsibility for the opinions he expressed. It is, of course, true that editorial opinion, as expressed in leading articles and so forth, was usually anonymous. That was a recognized convention; but if you read a particular paper, you knew who the editor was and you knew that he wrote his own editorials. To take an illustration, we may think of such a paper as *The Speaker* – the paper on which Chesterton began his journalistic career – which was taken over, round about the turn of the century, by a group of young Liberals with J. L. Hammond as editor. They wanted a platform from which they could express opinions that they believed to be true and important; and, according to their expert knowledge in different fields – foreign politics, labour relations, parliamentary affairs and the rest – they wrote regularly in the paper under their own names. The paper naturally included matter of general interest as well, such as book reviews, dramatic criticism, a financial page and, of course, a correspondence column in which many vigorous controversies were fought out. Apart from Hammond's editorials and the occasional article from a special correspondent, everything that appeared in the paper was signed.

In the 1900s and up to the First World War this kind of journalism was represented in a number of vigorously conducted weekly reviews such as the *New Statesman,* the *Athenaeum,* Orage's *New Age,* the *Saturday Review* and Cecil Chesterton's *New Witness;* it survived precariously into the inter-war period. But by the 1930s it was plain enough that independent journals of this kind could only be kept going at a loss, in other words by being subsidized. A number of them went bankrupt and disappeared; some survived by amalgamation and absorption into other organs; a few, of which *G. K.'s Weekly* was one, continued to run at a loss, kept in being at considerable personal expense to their directors.

With the popular newspapers it was, of course, quite different. By the time that Chesterton started in Fleet Street, all the national dailies were in rapid process of becoming large capitalist enterprises, conducted like any other large business concern and substantially dependent for their profits upon advertising revenue. Kennedy Jones, editor of *The Times*, once remarked to John Morley: 'You left journalism a profession; we have made it a branch of commerce.' And Chesterton himself has recalled how a newspaper proprietor lamented to him that there were still all these silly tales about ragged pressmen in Fleet Street and Bohemian parties in taverns and the rest. 'A newspaper office', he ended with a radiant smile, 'is now exactly like any other place of business.' It was a perfectly true statement. But the point is that, if it had been made any time before, say, 1900, it would have been bitterly resented by every journalist in Fleet Street as an insult to his profession. The journalist was, in fact, becoming a man who wrote things on the backs of advertisements.

'Read us', said the new popular newspapers – we are quoting a pleasantly satirical paragraph by the late Hamilton Fyfe – 'Read us and you will not be bothered by alarming revelations of fraud in business or incompetence in high places. We shall keep from you all disturbing news or at any rate tuck it away in inconspicuous corners. We want you to be easy in your mind, so that you may spend money freely. We owe it to our advertisers not to make you doubtful about the future or about anything. We shall stress the frivolous, diverting, unessential sides of life, so that you may feel cheerful and go out and buy things – preferably the things you see advertised in our pages. As for public evils and abuses, our motto is "Live and let live"; as for the poor, the best way is to pretend there aren't any.'*

That passage would, no doubt, need some difference of phrasing, or at any rate of emphasis, as applied to the present time. But it is a sufficiently accurate summary of the main journalistic tendencies during the first quarter of this century. A free press, in the old sense of the term, had almost disappeared. In his later years Chesterton could chuckle over his anomalous position as a *Daily News* columnist; but at the time he saw nothing humorous in it. He had joined the paper in 1902 as an enthusiastic young Liberal; he had canvassed for the Liberal Party in the general elections of 1902 and 1906. But he was never a real party man. The ideas and principles of Liberalism as a philosophy were one thing; but on a variety of practical questions – Church disestablishment, Free Trade, the reduction of armaments – his views were diametrically opposed to the official Liberal policy. And, apart altogether from this, he was becoming increasingly aware of the unreality and humbug of party politics as treated in the press.

'I remember', he wrote a good many years later, 'going to a great Liberal club, and walking about in a large crowded room, somewhere at the end of which a bald gentleman with a beard was reading something from a manuscript in a low voice. It was hardly unreasonable that we did not listen to him, because we could not in any case have heard; but I think a very large number of us did not even see him. We shifted and shunted about and collided with each other; I met various friends of mine and exchanged a few words; Bentley and Belloc and Hammond and the rest. We talked in an ordinary fashion; it is possible, though not certain, that one or other of us asked carelessly what was supposed to be happening in the other corner of the large hall. Then we drifted away together ... Next morning I saw across the front of my Liberal paper in gigantic headlines "Lord Spencer Unfurls the Banner".

* *The Highway*, November, 1931.

Under this were other remarks, also in large letters, about how he had blown the trumpet for Free Trade and how the blast would ring through England and rally all the Free-Traders. It did appear, on careful examination, that the inaudible remarks which the old gentleman had read from the manuscript were concerned with economic arguments for Free Trade; and very excellent arguments too, for all I know. But the contrast between what that orator was to the people who heard him, and what he was to the thousands of newspaper-readers who did not hear him, was so huge a hiatus and disproportion that I do not think I ever quite got over it.'*

That sort of experience could be amusing in retrospect. But in the early 1900s the older and finer traditions of journalism still survived – and Chesterton was an extremely unsophisticated young man when he first came to Fleet Street. The following years were to be for him years of an increasingly bitter disillusionment. As they went by, he saw the *Daily News*, as it seemed to him, jettisoning every principle of Liberalism at the dictation of the capitalist interests that controlled it. He saw Liberalism come to power, and that was quickly sufficient to destroy the last rags of his allegiance to the Liberal Party.

As with Belloc on the *Morning Post*, it was clear enough that his position on the *Daily News* was becoming an impossible one; the surprising thing was that it lasted as long as it did. In its columns he had vigorously attacked such Liberal measures as the Licensing Bill of 1908; he had denounced the first Unemployment Insurance Act as a decisive step towards the inauguration of the Servile State; he had criticized Liberal policy in education as a sentimental compromise that benefited nobody. Shaw had casually referred to him as 'that flourishing property of Mr. Cadbury', and the jest had certainly rankled. It may be true that the specific occasion of his final resignation from the *Daily News* was the publication in the *New Witness* of his well-known verses about the caddishness and vulgarity of cocoa; but the alliance had been an uneasy one for several years before that. He left the paper because it had come to stand for nearly everything with which he most violently

Autobiography, pp. 198–9.

disagreed and because he was sickened by what seemed to him the insincerity and venality of the new popular journalism. There is a fierce bitterness of spirit in the poem 'When I came back to Fleet Street', which he wrote about that time for the *New Witness*; it is a savage comment on the extinction of the old freedom of the press and the commercialization of the journalist's profession.

It is often supposed that the period immediately preceding the first Great War was one of easy calm and security, suddenly shattered by an almost unforeseen German aggression. The truth is far different. The end of the previous epoch, if such a thing can be discerned at all, might seem to have come with the death of Edward VII; the first three years of the reign of George V were as stormy and disturbed as any in our industrial history. There was still appalling poverty throughout the country. Drunkenness was a national vice whose effects on health and character were hideous beyond belief – 'we are justly renowned throughout the world', Chesterton once wrote, 'as the one specially and almost permanently drunken nation.' Time and again, between 1911 and 1914, the industrial life of the country was paralysed by strikes and lockouts, ruthlessly fought out on both sides. Troops were repeatedly called out to quell riots in London, Liverpool and other cities; in the railway strike of 1912, 57,000 regular soldiers were sent to different centres throughout the country and Haldane, as Minister of War, told the House that he doubted if they would be sufficient to maintain order. The suffragettes were pursuing their frenzied campaign of outrage and violence and masochism; and the government's attempts to deal with them were marked by some revolting excesses. There were frequent scenes in the House of Commons when all sense of dignity and order was lost, and members shouted abuse at one another across the floor. As to the general condition of public life, the parliamentary and journalistic career of the late Horatio Bottomley – the mere fact that such a career was possible – is a sufficient indication that Belloc's blisteringly satirical novels and his constant denunciation of political corruption were not very wide of the mark. The Marconi trial, as Robert Speaight judiciously says, gave little support to the thesis of collusion between the two front benches; but, at the very least, it left a nasty smell in the lobbies of the House of Commons.

The note of those years, in fact, was one of rising hysteria. It was as though the grievances, rivalries and disillusionments of a generation were mounting in a great tide of hatred, threatening the whole fabric of society. No man in touch with public life could remain unaffected by it; the prevailing mood was like an infection poisoning the national life.

Chesterton finally left the *Daily News* about the end of 1912. Almost at once he took the truly extraordinary step of joining the *Daily Herald*. It was especially an extraordinary step for him, since the main ground of his disgust with Liberal policy in action had been that it was an utter betrayal of Liberal principles and was in fact directed straight towards socialism, which in turn could only lead to the enslavement of the working classes under an all-powerful bureaucracy. He undoubtedly underestimated and misunderstood the tremendous popular impetus towards the socialist state; he certainly did not realize that the majority of his countrymen were already coming to regard security as a more desirable thing than freedom, nor did he then foresee the time when men would be imploring the State to deliver them from mere freedom, as from some terrible foreign oppressor. Perhaps he thought that, whatever he might find to disagree with in the policy of the *Daily Herald,* he might at least find some genuine idealism, some real concern for the welfare of the common man, rather less of the odious flattery of the rich, rather less readiness to accept the abominable assumption that poverty and unemployment were normally a man's own fault. If he thought any of these things, his disillusionment was to be even more bitter than anything that had gone before.

During his last years on the *Daily News* there had been a new note of violence in much of his political writing. More accurately than most men of his time he saw the way things were going in the national life, and he was appalled and bewildered by it. It seemed to him an evil and a crazy course that he was powerless to arrest. The strain of ten years of relentless overwork was beginning to tell. The Marconi case, with all its implications, was a far greater ordeal for him than for his more resilient brother, though the latter was the one directly concerned. And in Chesterton's weekly contributions to the *Daily Herald* one finds a shrillness, a lack of restraint, that make them, at times, almost terrifying to read, so obviously are they the work of a man overwrought to a dangerous degree. Already, one feels, there was upon him the shadow of the complete breakdown that struck him in the autumn of 1914, and nearly ended his life.

These *Daily Herald* articles are more recklessly violent than anything in the whole range of his journalism. There is in them no wit nor humour, no discussion of general ideas. Week after week he poured out fierce, sarcastic abuse of the Parliamentary Labour Party, of the Liberals and the Socialists, with bitter personalities about Lloyd George, Rufus Isaacs, the Webbs and such Labour leaders as Ramsay Macdonald and Arthur Henderson.

'Men in England are ruled at this minute by brutes who refuse them bread, by liars who refuse them news and by fools who cannot govern and therefore wish to enslave.'*

'If Mr Henderson wants to know what the Marconi scandal has saved us from, I can tell him. It has saved us from Socialism. My God! What Socialism, and run by what sort of Socialists! My God! What an escape!'†

Such language goes beyond the bounds of responsible criticism.

'There is no Liberal Party; there is no Unionist Party; there is no Labour Party. There is no such thing as individualism; there is no such thing as Socialism; there is no such thing as anti-Semitism. There is honesty and there is roguery; there is the fact and there is the official statement; there is death and there is deliverance ... there is nothing but a trumpet at midnight, calling for volunteers.'‡

A number of Chesterton's *Daily Herald* articles were brought together in a book called *The Utopia of Usurers*, which was published in America in 1917 – there was no English edition. It is not a book that adds anything to his reputation. There is in it a wildness of expression, a note sometimes rising almost to a scream,

---

* *Daily Herald*, April 15th, 1914.
† Ibid., December 21st, 1913.
‡ Ibid., May 24th, 1913.

that makes one realize how near he was coming to breaking-point in those immediately pre-war years; and if one studies the files of the paper as a whole during the time that he was writing for it, one sees, perhaps for the first time, what Robert Lynd meant when he said that, if Chesterton had not had in him a strain of angelic frivolity he could have become the blackest pessimist of his age. In this particular regard, there is a good deal in common between Chesterton and Ruskin. Both were men of unusually sensitive and generous human sympathy. Both were haunted and appalled almost to the point of madness by the malevolent anarchy of the social systems under which they lived. Like so many reformers, both allowed themselves to become obsessed with politics to a degree that was altogether disproportionate to their purposes and dangerous to the balance of their judgements. Both, faced by the hard and terrible facts of their time – poverty, unemployment, exploitation, corruption in high places and the rest – refused angrily to think in the vague terms and categories and the soothing clichés favoured by the politicians and professional sociologists. Both were well aware of a real peril to themselves – that, unless the reformer keeps himself closely in hand, he may in some sense, as Chesterton put it, catch something of the madness of the oppressors whom he is denouncing.

Chesterton has justly been called the poet and the prophet of the man in the street. He often said that there was no such thing as an average man; and scattered through his writings there are innumerable phrases that express his profound belief in the inalienable dignity of the individual person – 'the meanest man is immortal, but the mightiest movement is temporal': 'nothing is important but the fate of the soul' – any reader of Chesterton will recall similar expressions of the same basic belief. It was the starting-point of all that he had to say about the conditions under which men live and the proper purposes of political action and social reform, and it was the fundamental ground of his disagreement with his lifelong friend and antagonist, Bernard Shaw. For, as he saw it, the whole essence of Shaw's philosophy was that of a man utterly detached from human proceedings, unable to enter into the feelings and motives of ordinary people in spite of a genuine concern and zeal for their welfare. Shaw hated the poverty, squalor and overcrowding of the slums as violently as any man. He regarded physical suffering as the greatest of all evils but he could discuss such human tragedies as the loss of a man's faith or the break-up of his marriage with the most cheerful scepticism. He thought of human life in all its pathetic complexity in terms of problems for which you merely had to find the right solutions; and it was not surprising that his attitude to 'the poor' was one of contempt, as a race that did not deserve to survive.

To Chesterton's whole way of thinking this view was inhuman and pestilential. He, with his noble and perhaps over-romantic regard for the individual person and his profoundly Christian view of the meaning of poverty, would have knelt to wash the feet of a poor man. He could never detach himself from all the wrongs and evils that he saw around him in the national life. It tore him to pieces with what he called 'the perpetual torture of incompetent compassion' – a compassion that is so keenly expressed in such books as *What's Wrong with the World* and in such verses as *The Secret People* and *The Song of the Wheels*. Other reformers of the time were better able than he to think in theoretical terms and in the generalized formulae of planning and humanitarian effort; but Chesterton's sociology began, continued and ended with his affection and respect for 'the old, unaltered, fighting, beer-drinking, creed-making, child-loving, affectionate, selfish, unreasonable, respectable man'.* And, as he looked round at the forces of oppression and indifference and mistaken zeal that seemed to him to be robbing the common Englishman of the last vestiges of his dignity and freedom, there blazed in him an anger that came near to threatening the balance of his mind.

One thinks again of Ruskin. With him also, as the years went by, there came into his writing an increasing violence and bitterness, a mounting sense of evil, a conviction that the world was following a mad course that he was powerless to control. It was apparent to his friends, and he came to realize it himself, that if he was to keep his sanity, he must stop dwelling upon and writing about those subjects that so tortured him. Chesterton was never in so extreme

* *Daily News*, August 22nd, 1903.

a case as this. But there is this in common between the two men –
that they both had the range of thought and the power of will to
turn their minds, quite deliberately, away from the things of the
moment that so tormented them into more creative channels. It
was, no doubt, more difficult for Ruskin with his brooding, intro-
spective temperament than for Chesterton who was by nature so
genial and happy and high-spirited a person. But in both cases you
have the sense of a man freeing himself from a kind of bondage.
Ruskin turned from the tortured intensity of *Fors Clavigera* to
write again, in his own splendid manner, of pictures and mountains
and great literature; and you feel that he has recovered his real
self. In the same way, you can never feel that the Chesterton of the
savage, humourless *Daily Herald* articles is the real man at all.
Whilst those violently polemical articles were appearing week after
week, the real Chesterton was tossing off some of the best light
verse in the English language. And during that time he published
three books which, in their different ways, have probably given as
much pleasure as any that he ever wrote. They were *The Wisdom
of Father Brown,* which certainly contains some of the best stories
in the famous series; *The Victorian Age in Literature,* one of the
most stimulating surveys of that great period that has ever been
written, and perhaps the finest and most characteristic of all Chesterton's essays in literary criticism; and *The Flying Inn,* that
gloriously noisy extravaganza – resounding with noises of all
kinds from the braying of Pump's donkey and the growls of
Quoodle to the clash of arms in battle, the banging of beer-
tankards, the backfire of Dalroy's car and the tremendous roar of
his voice in speech and song – which perhaps owes its special
quality to the succession of magnificent songs whose echoes roll
over the English countryside as the Flying Inn pursues its way.*

When we look back over the period of about ten years between
the publication of *The Napoleon of Notting Hill* in 1904 and the
illness that struck him in the autumn of 1914, we are surely right
in regarding it, in a very real sense, as the great decade of his life.
If we agree with his own opinion that the *Napoleon* was his first

* Chesterton once said that, amongst all his books, the one that he had most
enjoyed writing was *The Flying Inn.*

serious book, we can regard its appearance as marking his achievement of full literary manhood. From this time onwards, all his
work, apart from his political journalism which was purely
ephemeral in purpose, was of one piece. His thought is developed
and matured as the years go by; but the development is
along an absolutely consistent line. There are few men of whom
this is true in anything like the same degree. And whilst it is
obvious that some of his best work belongs to his later years, it is
also true that he was never quite the same man after his illness
and that the sustained achievement of the pre-war decade – the
decade of *Heretics* and *Orthodoxy*, of the *Ballad of the White
Horse*, of the five full-length romances, of the *Charles Dickens*,
the first two volumes of *Father Brown*, of *The Victorian Age in
Literature* and much else shows him at the summit of his powers.

After the war Chesterton never again wrote regularly for any
national newspaper. He went on with his weekly essays in the
Illustrated London News and he was occasionally invited to write
a special article or contribute to symposiums in the daily press.
But in the new journalistic empires of post-war Fleet Street there
was no longer any place for the independent writer except in the
fields of literary and dramatic criticism and such-like. The essay
as a literary form was rapidly disappearing – Chesterton himself
and Robert Lynd were almost the last representatives of the long
tradition of English essay-writing. In the discussion of public
affairs, apart from the occasional commissioned article from an
expert, anonymity had already become the general practice and all
expression of opinion was controlled by the views or policy of the
proprietors. Chesterton's position had become anomalous enough
in the *Daily News* days; in the post-war set-up it would have been
impossible.

He had, of course, been associated with the *Eye Witness* and its
successor, the *New Witness*, since the paper's inception under
Belloc's editorship in 1911 – his brother had taken over from
Belloc in the following year when the name of the paper was
changed. But he had written surprisingly little in its columns and
had taken practically no part in its various campaigns, often conducted with reckless violence, against political corruption, social

injustice and the rest. Almost exclusively, his contributions were confined to light and satirical verse. All the songs in *The Flying Inn*, many of his ballades and some of his finest satirical pieces, such as 'The Revolutionist' and the more famous 'Anti-Christ, or the Reunion of Christendom', were first published in the *New Witness*. He used the paper as a sort of playground, turning away in odd moments from the tormenting realities of the contemporary scene to indulge in such glorious frivolities as the 'Ballade of Suicide' ('I think I will not hang myself today') and the 'Song against Grocers'.

The situation was entirely changed in 1916 when Cecil Chesterton joined the army and Gilbert took over the editorship. From that time onwards, with a brief gap of two years between the winding-up of the *New Witness* and the inauguration of *G. K.'s Weekly*, he was to remain an editor for the remaining twenty years of his life. After Cecil's death in a hospital in France he decided without hesitation that it was his duty and privilege to continue his brother's work; and in a sense it is true that the rest of his life was a sustained act of loyalty to his brother's memory. Some have said that *G. K.'s Weekly* killed him; there can be no doubt that it shortened his years – not so much by the actual amount of work involved (his capacity for work was almost inexhaustible), but simply because the conduct of the paper was an unremitting nightmare of anxiety.

In any discussion of Chesterton, there is bound to be difference of opinion about his journalistic work in general and about the whole episode of *G. K.'s Weekly* in particular. Was the thing worth while? Was he right to give so much of his time to political controversy and to matters of purely ephemeral importance? For many of us there was a time when we should have answered these questions in the affirmative, when the appearance of *G. K.'s Weekly* was a weekly stimulus and there was an infectious enthusiasm in the distributist movement and the newly founded League for the Restoration of Property, even if there was something of a 'let's pretend' atmosphere about it. In the early years the paper was read by a good many people who had no special interest in distributism but enjoyed Chesterton for his own sake. The book

THE MAN WHO WAS ORTHODOX

reviews and dramatic criticisms were lively and reliable. The paper was not very well edited; but Chesterton was too sensitive and conciliatory in personal relationships ever to be a successful editor. Still, it gave him once more an independent platform from which he could express his views about matters of public concern; his sister-in-law and Belloc, such old friends as Louis McQuilland and several younger men of ability wrote regularly. But the paper never came near to paying its way. As time went by, circulation and advertising revenue steadily declined, and *G. K.'s Weekly* became an increasing financial drain upon Chesterton himself and upon its other sponsors. There were disagreements on the staff which caused Chesterton a great deal of distress. Articles appeared for which apologies had to be made in the next issue. He himself saw clearly enough what was happening; the paper in Robert Speaight's words was becoming 'a platform with too many cranks addressing too many cliques in a hall that was never more than half full'.*

To read through the later files of *G. K.'s Weekly* is not an exhilarating task. You can see, coming into all Chesterton's advocacy, an increasing note of fatigue and despondency. You have the increasing sense of a tired man to whom the writing of a 1,500-word editorial and a 2,000-word middle-page article week after week (and he scarcely ever wrote less) has become an almost intolerable effort. His vision of the world around him was as clear as ever, especially in the international field; but his political comments on home affairs had lost a good deal of their relevance and we think it is true that he curiously misconceived the nature of the social revolution that was taking place in this country. Meanwhile, the paper had to come out and he must go on writing. Some journalist or other, scribbling for dear life in Fleet Street, would make some inconceivably silly remark about the Emancipation of Youth or the Future of the Churches or some such topic. And G.K. would pick it up and play with it and turn it upside down and make it look even more idiotic than it really was – and it was all very diverting, but what waste of time and effort for a mind like his! Little of what he wrote in the paper during the last seven or

* *The Life of Hilaire Belloc,* p. 482.

eight years of his life has been reprinted; and the reason is plain enough – there was very little that was worth reprinting. In the present collection it will be found that there are not many passages taken from the later volumes of *G. K.'s Weekly*.*

It is obvious enough that, if Chesterton had given less time to purely ephemeral journalism, he would probably have written more books of permanent value than he actually did. The fact may be regretted. We would give a great deal to have had from him the books on Savonarola and on Shakespeare that he planned to write for so many years – the former was more than once announced by Hodder and Stoughton as being 'in preparation'. There was a fortunate gap of two years between the end of the *New Witness* and the beginning of *G. K.'s Weekly*; and it was during that time, with his mind free of editorial responsibilities, that he wrote what is certainly one of his best-loved books and what is equally certainly one of his most important – the *St Francis of Assisi* and *The Everlasting Man*.

But to wish that he had been less of a journalist is merely to wish that he had been a different person from what he was; and, as we have said, Chesterton was first and foremost a journalist. It was in his nature to live in the day-to-day stress of the world around him. All his life he fought for the freedom and dignity and the ordinary loyalties and the elementary rights of the common man. He fought in the light of perfectly clear principles and made no concessions to the shifting moods of public opinion. Near the end of his life he said that he had never taken his books very seriously, but he had always taken his beliefs very seriously indeed. He was quite indifferent to any evidences of success or influence. He just went on writing for any who might choose to listen to him, convinced that 'in the end it will not matter to us whether we wrote well or ill; but it will greatly matter on which side we fought'. As Professor Emile Cammaerts put it, he wrote his books and his articles as a ploughman ploughs his field.

'Every page was a new furrow; when he had reached the end of

---

* It must be remembered, of course, that *G.K.'s Weekly* has been fairly well quarried. Much of Chesterton's best work in it is to be found in such books as *The Outline of Sanity*, *The Thing*, and *The Well and the Shallows*.

it, he turned his horses' heads against the wind and started another, indifferent to the weather, grateful for the birds which accompanied his track. He never paused to sing a song; he sang as he went along. His poetry preserved the perfect rhythm of his walk. He was often compelled to stop to remove the stones which obstructed his way. Each of his essays marked a new effort to prepare the ground for the rake and the seed. When he was too tired to go on ploughing, he sat under a hedge at the top of the hill and surveyed the landscape of his memory and dreamed of Browning and Dickens and Cobbett and Francis and Thomas – of all those who, by deed or word, had helped to keep his furrows straight.'*

It is to Chesterton's honour that he steadfastly resisted the temptation – which must have been a powerful one at certain times in his life – to pull out of the cockpit of political and social controversy and all that it involved, and to become purely a man of letters. It is to his honour that, being the man he was, he chose to remain a journalist to the end of his days. And, when considering his work as a whole, we must not forget how many of his books, including some of his best, were simply collected journalism. All the books of essays, all his short stories, a good deal of his verse and such books as *The Superstition of Divorce, Irish Impressions*, and *The Outline of Sanity* appeared first in various newspapers, reviews and magazines.

What may legitimately be regretted is that he involved himself so continuously in purely ephemeral controversies and was drawn, largely under the influence of his brother and Belloc, into a type of polemical journalism in which they excelled, but for which he was quite unsuited. Chesterton was a magnificent advocate and an extremely skilled debater; but he was not cut out for mere controversy of whatever kind. A fairly thick skin; a not too sensitive conscience; an extreme accuracy in the use of facts and figures; a sense of expediency; an understanding of the arts of compromise and accommodation; a readiness to make enemies and to harry them relentlessly; an acute ear for gossip – these are some of the qualities needed for effectiveness in this kind of journalism. None of them are qualities that one associates with Chesterton.

* *The Laughing Prophet*, p. 201.

But quite apart from this, he lived much too exclusively in the world of ideas to be effective in most matters of public controversy. No one excelled him in the clear-cut statement of principle, the drawing of the sharp distinction between the essentials and incidentals of a disputed question. But practical problems – the sort of problems on which wide variety of opinion is possible – are seldom solved by mere insistence on principle or the mere application of logical thought. All kinds of factors and circumstances, material as well as human, have to be taken into account; and it was here that Chesterton so often failed as a controversialist. The subject is one on which a good deal might be said, but a single illustration will perhaps suffice.

Everyone who knows Chesterton has enjoyed his drinking-songs and most of us are duly amused by his praise of beer and public-houses and conviviality and the rest of it. That kind of thing was perhaps a bit overdone; it certainly annoyed the puritanically-minded, and Shaw once asked in exasperation – 'Have I survived the cry of Art for Art's sake and of War for War's sake, for which Mr Chesterton rebukes Whistler and Mr Rudyard Kipling, to fall a victim to this maddest of all cries: the cry of Beer for Beer's sake?'*

But even if one agrees with Shaw that all the talk about beer was sometimes silly and irresponsible, there was no need to take it too seriously. It was all done with a sort of noisy bravado, a humorous defiance of the teetotallers and the nonconformist conscience; and it would be absurd to take the songs in *The Flying Inn*, for example, as solemn encouragements to alcoholic excess.

But there was a more serious side to the matter. In the 1900s drunkenness was unquestionably the greatest single cause of poverty, crime and lunacy in the country. At that time it is hardly an exaggeration to say that the licensing laws were such as to permit the maximum of temptation to drunkenness with the maximum of opportunity. Up till 1914 the public houses in London were open from five o'clock in the morning till half an hour after midnight. Bar-tending was one of the worst of the sweated trades and had one of the highest mortality rates from alcoholism. The

* *The Nation*, August 28th, 1909.

'Trade' had immense political influence and was violently opposed to all efforts towards reform. It needed the national emergency of war to bring in, under the Defence of the Realm Act, the first curtailment of the hours of opening. All the efforts of the great temperance reformers from Gladstone and Cardinal Manning onwards had been powerless to break the reactionary policy of the brewers and distillers; the Licensing Bill of 1908, which stirred the imagination and fired the enthusiasm of all concerned with this hideous national problem, got through the Commons with a substantial majority, but was thrown out by the Lords.

Chesterton's attitude to this great question was rigidly consistent; it was also inept, unrealistic and quite deplorable. He took his stand on the principle that a man's habits in eating and drinking were his own affair; any attempt by superior authority to prevent him from drinking whatever he wanted and whenever he wanted it was an interference with personal liberty and therefore to be violently resisted. Drink, he declared, is a peril which each man must face and control for himself. Consequently, he denounced the temperance movement, with its desperate concern to grapple in some way with the appalling condition of affairs, as a mere campaign by rich faddists to meddle with the poor. He was content to associate it with puritanism and cocoa and political hypocrisy and fussy philanthropy and other things that he disliked, and to leave it at that. He opposed the Licensing Bill on the absurd grounds that the proposal to shorten the hours of opening was some kind of brewers' ramp to make people so crowded and uncomfortable in the public houses that they would swallow their drinks more quickly and so consume more. He attacked the Children's Act of 1910, which forbade young children in public houses, saying that the measure could be a prelude to excluding them from bookshops, butchers' shops and other sorts of shop.

His attitude, in fact, was precisely that of those theorists and cranks whom he justly criticized for seizing on a particular idea or principle – in this case the liberty of the individual – isolating it from other highly relevant principles and being led to conclusions that were perverse and, as most of us must believe, wrong. It would be just as legitimate (and as ridiculous) to argue that, since every citizen has a right to use the public highway, any legislation which seeks to make the roads safer by imposing speed limits, controlling traffic, insisting on driving tests and so forth, is a monstrous interference with liberty. The truth is, of course, that the liberty of the individual is rightly and necessarily limited by his membership of society; it is inevitable and proper that, where the public good is manifestly concerned, there should be some sacrifice of private freedom.

The plain fact is that there were certain questions with which Chesterton never seemed able to deal open-mindedly, and this was one of them. During the First World War one of his admirers wrote to him:

'I do beg you, Mr Chesterton, much as you love writing about drink, to give it a rest during the war. ... You may have the degradation of any number of silly boys to your account without knowing it.'*

It was a charge, as his biographer says with delicate meiosis, that he never quite answered. We are not sure that he ever attempted to answer it. In this matter, about which he never altered his opinions in the smallest degree, his humane and compassionate judgement, his profound understanding of human frailty, his intense concern for better social conditions – all seem to have been averted from the realities, the terrible realities, of things as they were. It is true that his denunciation of the prohibitionist experiment in post-war America followed logically from what he had been saying for years about affairs in England. But his arguments on that subject were more carefully reasoned; and, anyhow, prohibition had never been a serious issue in this country. One can admire the courage and public spirit that kept him in the controversial arena all through his active life. And if one regrets the time and the effort that it cost him, it is chiefly because one feels that there were so many other things that he did so much better. The real point is that Chesterton was far too much of a creative thinker to be at the same time a practical reformer.

* Ward, p. 324.

III

Ruskin says somewhere that for a hundred people who can feel there is only one who can think; but for ten thousand who can think there is only one who can see. His meaning is clear enough. He is speaking of that rare power of intuition which is called in scripture the gift of wisdom – an immediate apprehension of truth that outstrips the exercise of reason, coming like a sudden blaze of light and with a quality of revelation. It is expressed sometimes in a single sentence, sometimes in a paragraph or in a whole book, and perhaps most often in poetry. Ruskin had this gift himself. George Macdonald had it; and Chesterton certainly had it too.

'When you break the big laws, you do not get liberty; you do not even get anarchy. You get the small laws.'*

Or again –

'The meanest man is immortal and the mightiest movement is temporal, not to say temporary.'†

Or again, on the subject of suffering –

'The King may be conferring a decoration when he pins the man on the cross, as much as when he pins the cross on the man.'‡

A man might remember his first readings of such passages as decisive events in his life. They produce precisely that effect of shock or surprise which, as Chesterton repeatedly insisted, is necessary to awaken us to see things as they really are, to see the world with a proper astonishment and a proper gratitude. In most people that sense is awakened only in rare moments of excitement or exaltation; in many it is never awakened at all.

Chesterton thought, not only that truth must always be surprising, but that surprise is an essential element in any great human experience. He constantly annoyed his critics by his apparent delight in inverting the commonplace, standing the proverb on its head (as when he says that 'if a thing is worth doing at all, it is

* *Daily News*, July 29th, 1905.
† *Blackfriars*, January, 1923.
‡ *Illustrated London News*, February 10th, 1906.

worth doing badly', which is in fact the amateur's *magna carta* and a necessary incentive to all creative effort), or developing an argument from the exact opposite of a commonly accepted premise. But his purpose in doing this kind of thing was never frivolous; it was rather what the artist does when he turns his picture upside down in order to judge whether the balance of the composition and the basic values are right. You must see the familiar things in an unfamiliar way. You must make all things new. It is only in that innocence of vision that the essential truth is to be discerned.

You must approach the familiar thing by unfamiliar ways. That is why Innocent Smith travels round the world, through the steppes of Russia and the forests of China and the mountain villages of California, to find his way home; he breaks into his own house through the skylight to discover what his own house is really like; he elopes time and again with his own wife, simply to renew the sense of her perpetual value and the splendour of their married love. This idea of all journeying as a homeward journey and all vision as a recovery of surprise occurs again and again in Chesterton's thought – in *Orthodoxy*, in *The New Jerusalem*, in his poems and in a number of his essays. It haunted his mind to the end of his life.

Of course he was misunderstood. It was always easy to dismiss him as a mere buffoon or, at best, an ingenious pedlar of paradoxes. He irritated a great many people and embarrassed many others by his habit of, as they expressed it, dragging religion into everything that he wrote. After all, you expected to find religious questions discussed in theological books and periodicals, and you could read them if you wished. But what were you to make of a man who seemed unable to write a book about Dickens or a casual essay on policemen without plunging into discussions about miracles or the doctrine of original sin? It was the more disconcerting that he insisted on writing of these essentially solemn questions in breezy, colloquial language, seasoned with scintillating humour, as though they were matters of general interest or at least of some concern to ordinary people.

These complaints were understandable, and the truth is simple enough. Chesterton was one of the few great English men of letters to whom the Christian religion was an all-embracing philosophy to which nothing could be irrelevant. Leaving aside his purely ephemeral journalism it can be said of him that, in the whole range and variety of his literary expression, he was never concerned with anything less than the ultimate meaning and purpose of life. This quality became more marked as he grew older, but it was apparent all through his mature life. To take a random instance, you can read *The Man Who Was Thursday* as an excellent piece of story-telling on an ingenious theme. As pure entertainment it is as good as anything that Chesterton ever wrote. But, as the well-known dedication to E. C. Bentley makes clear, it is a book with a very definite purpose. It was written as a counterblast to the pessimism of Schopenhauer and the decadents and it is concerned with the elementary truth that, on the whole, the universe is a friendly place and not a mere bear-garden of meaningless conflict. In the context of the story, a man who thinks himself the only policeman in a world of anarchy is on the straight road to insanity, until he realizes that most of his supposed enemies are in fact his friends and allies.

The second and more profound theme that runs through all the fun and high spirits of the narrative, centres on the immense symbolic figure of Sunday, the mysterious and boisterous president of the anarchist group. In the penultimate chapter of the book, when the ex-anarchists sit talking about him, it becomes apparent that each of them is describing him quite differently. None feels that he has ever seen or known Sunday as he really is. Each one of them, as it were, has been living in a world of his own – a world that cannot be fully understood, a world that can appear chaotic and purposeless. Each of them had the sense that he had never seen the face of Sunday, but only his back – like a man looking at the back of a tapestry and unable to see the picture on the other side. Yet somehow the belief persists that, in the fulness of an apprehension beyond human attainment at present, there is in the order of creation a harmony to which all things contribute. And in the last vision of *The Man Who Was Thursday* some hint is shown of the reconciliation of the world in a divine act of redemption.

To Chesterton there could be no question of dragging religion into matters with which it had no connection. He would have denied, and repeatedly did deny, that religion was a self-contained department of thought like economics or biochemistry. That proposition could only be true if religion were a matter of investigation and induction like any other purely human field of inquiry. As soon as the question of revelation is introduced, the situation becomes entirely different.

'You cannot,' he said, 'evade the issue of God: whether you talk about pigs or the binomial theory, you are still talking about Him. ... If Christianity should happen to be true – that is to say, if its God is the real God of the universe – then defending it may mean talking about anything and everything. Things can be irrelevant to the proposition that Christianity is false, but nothing can be irrelevant to the proposition that Christianity is true. Zulus, gardening, butchers' shops, lunatic asylums, housemaids and the French Revolution – all these things not only may have something to do with the Christian God, but must have something to do with Him if He lives and reigns.'*

There was plenty of good Christian apologetic being produced in Edwardian England, but it made little impact on the ordinary reading public because it was written, naturally and properly enough, in the language of theology and had a specifically 'religious' flavour and intention. Most of it was essentially defensive, and Chesterton from the first struck an entirely different note. Here, writing regularly in the secular press on all kinds of topics, was a Christian apologist who possessed a great skill in debate, an exuberant wit, a keener understanding of the minds of his opponents than they had themselves, and a sound equipment as a practical theologian – an apologist, too, who was by no means content with a strategy of defence. On the contrary, he was concerned to show, as the starting-point of his counter-offensive, that Christianity provided the only sane explanation of the universe and that the Christian life, so far from being a stuffy, outmoded system of vetos and restrictions, was a great adventure in possession of the truth that can alone make a man free. He was

* *Daily News*, December 12th, 1903.

further concerned to show that the articles of orthodox Christian belief had an immediate and most practical relevance to the whole ordering of human life.

There were times when he weakened his advocacy by reckless overstatement; he acknowledged that he was always apt to state his opinions with unnecessary violence, partly through sheer intellectual pugnacity and partly through always writing in a hurry. Like Shaw and Blatchford and other contemporaries, he was certain that, if you want to get people to listen to you, you must begin by startling them. If you intended to discuss any aspect of the Christian religion, it was useless to take your stand on the platform of pious exhortation and cautious defence. You must first get back to the elemental idea of what religion is.

Chesterton believed that, if religion is anything at all – if, in particular, it is anything more than a dull convention of self-righteousness – it must be recognized as something normal to man and as one of the most powerful forces that have shaped his destiny. The religious impulse is rooted in human nature and in that sense the Christian revelation may be considered as the authentic answer to an agelong quest or nostalgia. Obviously the various provinces of man's thought and activity have their own autonomies; but it was a special characteristic of the age in which Chesterton grew up that many of those autonomies had become absolute and irresponsible. The result had been a disastrous fragmentation of life and personality wherein religion, politics, family life and so forth had become separate provinces, marked by inviolable frontiers and directed by different and often inconsistent standards. Any proper integration, as Chesterton saw it, could only come about by recovering the original unity of the religious idea.

To the literary and journalistic world of the time this kind of thing was entirely bewildering. The mere idea of any serious defence of Christian orthodoxy seemed grotesque. And when Chesterton first began to discuss these matters, the effect was one of stunned astonishment. He had a greater power than most of his contemporaries for saying exactly what he meant. But what he said, and went on saying, appeared manifestly absurd; the only

44

conclusion was that he could not really mean it. The thing was a pose or a stunt or some kind of incomprehensible joke.

This attitude was to pursue Chesterton all through his life; it may have been partly his own fault because his humour could often become a tiresome facetiousness. It is anyhow certain that in those early years there were few who could take him seriously. He once remarked that he only made jokes to make himself laugh and to relieve the intolerable tedium of trying to tell the truth. His real concern was to defy the conventions of a joyless Puritanism that had separated laughter from so many of the most important things in life. Of course it is obvious that there are circumstances and occasions where humour would be utterly out of place; at the same time, there is no subject so inherently solemn or serious that it is wrong to make jokes about it. 'Life is serious all the time, but living cannot be serious all the time.'

When Chesterton first started writing, it was as though he had invented a new idiom which few could understand. There had been plenty of humour and wit and ridicule in public controversy on religious matters, but it had all been on the other side – everyone took for granted the ridiculing of tradition and orthodoxy. The idea of using such weapons in their defence was so novel as to be almost incomprehensible. In retrospect, it is possible to discuss Chesterton from many points of view, for he was one of the most many-sided writers that has ever lived. But his primary importance lies, not only in the ideas that he expressed, but in the astonishing originality with which he expressed them. One of his chief titles to renown is that he was by far the most powerful and influential Christian apologist of his time. There must be many Christian people alive today – most of them probably middle-aged by now – who, humanly speaking, owe their faith to him.

*　　　*　　　*

This does not mean that he is to be thought of primarily as a theologian or even that his writings on specifically religious themes were necessarily his most important. Comparatively little of his work was in the strict sense theological. What mattered – what gave the power and the special character to all that he had to say –

was the belief, illustrated in every book that he ever wrote, that a sane and true theology is the necessary framework of any satisfactory way of life. He first found that theology summarized in the granite formulae of the Nicene Creed. And during the early years of this century he was the only important English writer – the only writer, that is, of anything like the same genius or with anything approaching the same appeal – whose work was informed through and through by a belief in Christian orthodoxy.

It was, of course, part of his strength that he did not come to this belief until he was nearly thirty; and when he looked back in middle age on the main currents of thought in his lifetime, it seemed to him, as he put it, that his literary life had lasted from a time when men were losing happiness by despair to a time when they were losing it by presumption. It is difficult enough to generalize about the most significant trends of thought in any age, and especially so in a period so rich and varied in expression as the 1890s. But it is certainly true that the dominant note of the most representative literature of those years – a note sounded with many differing degrees of emphasis and reference – was one of disillusionment and even despair. Chesterton summed it up in lines that have often been quoted:

> A cloud was on the mind of men, and wailing went the weather,
> Yea, a sick cloud upon the soul when we were boys together.
> Science announced nonentity and art admired decay;
> The world was old and ended: but you and I were gay;
> Round us in antic order their crippled vices came –
> Lust that had lost its laughter, fear that had lost its shame.
> Like the white lock of Whistler, that lit our aimless gloom,
> Men showed their own white feather as proudly as a plume.
> Life was a fly that faded, and death a drone that stung;
> The world was very old indeed when you and I were young.*

It was a time when Schopenhauer was declaring that the will to live is a sort of snare that keeps us living against all right reason. Housman was asking why he had been woken up to live and how soon he might die and go to sleep again. Swinburne, with what

* Dedication of *The Man Who Was Thursday*.

Chesterton called his 'queer licentious pessimism', compared life to a dreary river that does at last drag its tortuous course down to the sea of death. Amongst the younger poets, John Davidson expressed the same bitterness of spirit, sometimes with a certain dignity and beauty, but often in mere petulant cynicism.

All this *malaise* was ultimately rooted in theology and followed directly from the breakdown of Victorian Protestantism under the impact of the new scientific knowledge. For many who stood in the old traditions it had been a bewildering disintegration of beliefs in which they had grown up and which they regarded as stable and imperishable. They were like men moving blindly in a great cloud of dust following a landslide. Victorian biographies abound in narratives of this kind of religious shipwreck. They make tragic reading, with the same *motif* occurring again and again – a Christian upbringing, usually Anglican; the sudden or gradual impact of knowledge or ideas that cannot be assimilated; the stress and conflict of mind ending in the loss of every belief that had given life its meaning; and then the agonizing effort to rebuild something upon the ruins.

As a young man Chesterton had seen the effects of all this very clearly. He had not himself been brought up in the traditions of the older orthodoxy, and in that sense he could see the tragedy objectively.

'To many men of that time', he wrote in one of his early essays, 'had happened the most black and hopeless catastrophe conceivable to human nature; they had found a logical explanation of all things. To them it seemed that an Ape had suddenly risen to gigantic stature and destroyed the seven heavens. ... It has been constantly supposed that they were angry with Darwinism because it appeared to do something or other to the Book of Genesis; but this was a pretext or fancy. They fundamentally rebelled against Darwinism because they had a fear, not altogether unreasonable or unfounded, that it would affect morality. Man had been engaged, through innumerable ages in a struggle with sin. But in this struggle he had always had nature on his side. He might be polluted and agonized, but the flowers were innocent and the hills were strong. ... [This seemed] the hour when, to all mortal

47

appearances, the whole of the physical world deserted to the devil.'*

It seemed, in fact, that nature was no more than a brutal and purposeless mechanism and that the idea of a God who was in any sense immanent in his creation was a superstition now decisively exploded. About all this, in its popularized forms, there appeared a complete finality. The uncertainty and vulnerability of the Darwinian theory was not even imagined; and it is curious to note that the most spirited attacks on Darwinism came, not from Christian protagonists, but from disinterested parties like Samuel Butler who were quite unconcerned with the religious issues.

All this welter of disillusionment and pessimism was a kind of nemesis of Victorian Calvinism. It found its noblest and most tragic expression in the writings of Thomas Hardy, that good and gracious and humble man who loved and understood his fellows so profoundly and reviled the malevolent gods that ruled their destinies. In his late 'teens and early twenties Chesterton had been too near the abyss himself to be insensitive to the horrible plausibility of these ideas. But he never for a moment lost the instinct of revolt against them. He never lost the elemental conviction that the world was a place worth living in and that, as he remembered hearing his grandfather declare, a man should thank God for his creation, even if he knew he was a lost soul.

In the intellectual world in which Chesterton grew up, agnosticism had become an established thing. There was an agnostic orthodoxy, a uniformity of unbelief, which was found not merely amongst 'advanced' people, but among educated people as a whole. When Chesterton started going round lecturing to the various groups and societies – Ethical Societies, Higher Thought Centres and so on – which abounded in the London suburbs, he made the natural assumption that each society was a coherent body or congregation of people brought together by a common belief of one kind or another – that a Theosophical Society consisted of people who assembled because they all believed in theosophy; that an Ethical Society meant a group of people who believed in ethics without the sanctions of revealed religion, and so forth. It

* 'Tennyson', by G. K. Chesterton and Richard Garnett. (Bookman Booklets 1903; reprinted in *A Handful of Authors*.)

took him some time to realize that the facts were quite different. He first noticed that the same people were often to be found in a variety of different congregations. He found that, whilst there might be a real feeling of loyalty to a particular leader or preacher who presided over this or that group, there seemed little indication of any unity of belief or practice. Only one thing was common to every society and every group, and that was the convention of dissent from orthodoxy, the convention of 'not going to church'. The truth of the whole matter did not strike him till long afterwards.

'I believe now', he wrote many years later, 'that the congregations of these semi-secular chapels consist largely of one vast and vague sea of wandering doubters, with their wandering doubts, who may be found one Sunday seeking a solution from the Theists and another Sunday from the Theosophists ... There never were any large schools of thought, so separate and so static as I innocently imagined in my youth. I have been granted, as it were, a sort of general view or vision of all that field of negation and groping and curiosity. And I saw pretty much what it all really meant. There was no Theistic Church; there was no Theosophical Brotherhood; there were no Ethical Societies; there were no New Religions. But I saw Israel scattered on the hills as sheep that have not a shepherd; and I saw a large number of the sheep run about bleating eagerly in whatever neighbourhood it was supposed that a shepherd might be found.'*

In his autobiography and elsewhere Chesterton has described how he laboured his way through this jungle of doubt, first to the kind of elemental optimism to be learnt from such writers as Stevenson, Whitman and Browning, and finally, under the influence of his wife and such friends as Conrad Noel, Percy Dearmer and Rann Kennedy, to the full acceptance of Christianity. His conversion – for it was no less – was not a sudden one; it was a steady process of illumination and discovery spread over the period of his courtship and early married life. 'It was,' he said, 'in Notting Hill and Battersea that I began to see that Christianity is true.'

* *Autobiography*, pp. 173, 175.

In this process, as in the whole course of his life, the quiet, sympathetic influence of his wife cannot be overestimated. Amongst his friends, it is probable that the most influential was Conrad Noel, then a curate at St Mary Magdalene's, Paddington.

Noel was an aristocrat by birth and a rebel by instinct – he appears recognizably in *Manalive* as the Rev. Henry Percy. He cultivated surprising eccentricities of dress and could, as the mood took him, look like an artist straight out of Chelsea or a Newmarket trainer. When he wore clerical clothes, he often affected a kind of furry cap which, as Chesterton said, gave him the appearance of an aesthetic rat-catcher. Certainly, it would have been impossible to imagine anyone less like the stage curate of *The Private Secretary* with his Bath bun and his goloshes. Noel was a true zealot; there burned in him a fiery devotion to the Catholic tradition in the Church of England and to the cause of Christian Socialism, the latter in a far more radical form than that represented by such men as Gore and Scott Holland.

Chesterton and Noel started meeting at various debating societies of which they were both members, and there was one thing that Chesterton soon noticed with surprise. In all these debates it was common to find the keenest interest in the actual process of discussion, but very little ability or even desire to reach conclusions. The only people of whom this did not seem to be true were the clergy. It was certainly not true of Noel; nor was it true of Cartmel Robinson, Vicar of Chiswick, who often came to meetings of the I.D.K. club in Bedford Park – a society whose name might prompt the question, 'What does I.D.K. stand for?' to which one off-handedly replied, 'I don't know'. Anyhow, these clergymen did, at least, seem to recognize the fact that the human mind is an instrument for coming to conclusions, and that debate and discussion should have no other purpose than that.

'Having myself', wrote Chesterton, 'been trained, first on the farce about the curate, and then on the scepticism about the priest, I was quite ready to believe that a dying superstition was represented by such feeble persons. As a fact, I found that they were very often by far the ablest and most forcible persons. In debate after debate I noticed the same thing happen . . . It was the farcical curate, it was the feeble-minded clergyman, who got up and applied to the wandering discussion at least some sort of test of some sort of truth; who showed all the advantages of having been tolerably trained in some sort of system of thinking. . . . It seemed to me that the despised curates were rather more intelligent than anyone else; that they, alone in that world of intellectualism, were trying to use their intellects.'*

Meanwhile, the plain fact remained that the breakdown of the old orthodoxies had left a vacuum which neither the Church nor any of the denominations had been able to fill. Most educated people identified historic Christianity, not only with political reaction, but with a discredited theology and an outmoded moral code. They knew nothing of the work of the great Anglican, Roman Catholic and Nonconformist scholars, who were re-establishing the authority of scripture on a firm basis. They were untouched by the rising vigour alike of the catholic and evangelical movements in the Church of England. The older techniques of evangelism meant nothing to them.

At that time (that is, about the turn of the century) a group of earnest Christian thinkers were voicing their belief that what was needed was a re-statement of Christianity in the light of modern knowledge, a 'New Theology' which would reconcile the claims of science and religion. With a naïve confidence in what they thought the unchallengeable finality of contemporary scientific conclusions, they believed that this could only be done by bringing theology into line with them. That was really the starting-point of the so-called modernist movement – not, of course, at the level of serious scholarship, but in relation to popular apologetic.

In this country the movement was mainly nonconformist in origin. Most of the leading exponents of the 'new theology' were nonconformist ministers; the most prominent was the Rev. R. J. Campbell, then a Congregationalist, who was drawing crowds to the City Temple on Sunday after Sunday in the early 1900s. Much of his teaching was perfectly orthodox. It was in their attempt to

* *Autobiography*, p. 159.

reconcile evolutionary theory with Christian belief that he and the other 'new theologians' ran into difficulties.

The Darwinian theory of evolution sought to explain the modification of species through geological time by the agency of natural selection – or, as it came to be called, the survival of the fittest. As popularized at the journalistic level, the theory seemed to show that nature, so far from reflecting the beneficence of its creator, was the theatre of a ruthless conflict with the destruction of the weak as its primary law. This was the legacy which man, with his animal ancestry, had inherited. All human conflict, all the wars and massacres of the past, all the rubs and quarrels in human relationships, were but the fruits of this heritage. Man still had the ape and the tiger in him.

To this interpretation of the historical process the New Theologians found an answer in the idea of progress. They pointed out that the evidence of history showed that, on the whole, the world was getting better. Manners were becoming more refined, barbarism was giving way to civilization, and so forth. The human story did reveal a slow but steady ascent towards fuller and higher and better ways of life.

From this it followed that the traditional Christian doctrine of the Fall of Man, of original sin, of the very existence of evil in any positive sense, was out of line with assured scientific conclusions. Man could and would perfect himself by his own effort. What was called sin was simply the vestige of his animal origin. In its essence the New Theology was a generous revolt against the very Calvinism which had been integral to the nonconformist tradition in the Victorian age. But a theology which implicitly denied the relevance of any doctrine of redemption was no restatement of revealed truth. It was something quite alien to any interpretation of Christian belief.

Chesterton was never quite fair to the modernist movement as a whole. In his later years he was too inclined to equate it with the journalistic vagaries of men like Bishop Barnes and Dean Inge. He often gave an impression of impatience with serious scholarship. He was too ready to make silly jokes about dons and he had a lot of fun at one time and another with the biblical critics – the spoof *Hibbert Journal* article in *The Flying Inn* is one of the most genuinely funny things he ever wrote. He always seemed to think of modernists as perverse, provocative people with one-track minds who delighted in attacking some hitherto unquestioned truth, especially where the Bible was concerned. What he failed to see in any sort of perspective was the immense revolution that was taking place in the whole field of biblical study. And what he failed to realize was that the new biblical scholarship, so far from weakening the authority of scripture, was re-establishing that authority on a firmer basis than had ever before been possible.

Nevertheless, he made no mistake about the New Theology. As a journalist, Chesterton was always concerned with ideas at what may be called the popular level – the level at which the cautious conclusions of the specialist have usually become sensationalized and misinterpreted by self-styled experts. What he rightly objected to in the New Theology was that it was not founded upon assured scientific knowledge, but upon an ill-digested jumble of hypothesis and guesswork – 'a great mass of hazy and half-educated evolutionism' which no scientist of repute would have accepted for a moment. And when the New Theologians declared that their aim was a reconciliation of Christianity with modern thought, Chesterton's reply was that, on the contrary, it was for modern thought to examine itself in sackcloth and ashes that it might come to terms with Christianity.

Well, we have no difficulty nowadays in recognizing that history shows no upward progression towards a coming millennium. The existence of evil as a malignant infection afflicting the whole world is evident enough today. This was the point on which Chesterton found the New Theology most vulnerable. Evil or sin or whatever you like to call it was so obvious and enormous a reality that any religion which failed to accept it and try to explain it could hardly expect to be listened to. You could not just by-pass it, which was what the New Theology was doing.

Chesterton had a good deal to say at one time and another about the New Theology, and his first concern was to point out that the only satisfactory, and indeed the only cheerful explanation of the problem of evil was the Christian doctrine of the Fall.

That was what needed re-stating in plain terms that everyone could understand.

'The true doctrine of original sin', he wrote, 'may be stated in a million ways, like every very central and solid truth. You may put it this way; that moral health is not a thing which fulfils itself automatically like physical health. Or this way: that we all start in a state of war. Or this way: that everything in a cabbage is trying to make a good cabbage, whereas everything in a man is not trying to make what we call a good man. Or this way: that virtue is a creditable thing and not, like the greenness of a cabbage, merely an admirable thing.'*

In another context he pointed out that you could look at the matter in still another way if you consider Aristotle's principle of the golden mean. Man in this world is constantly, a hundred times a day, losing and trying to recover his balance. Often he slips and, by a frantic effort towards equilibrium, recovers himself. If he falls, he will not be content to stay on the ground – some instinct of dignity or self-consciousness will bring him reeling to his feet.

'This life of ours and the great pathway of history and civilization is a road entirely carpeted with orange peel. The obstacles are so numerous, the complications are so varied, that we live, as it were, in an eternal crisis, in an immortal catastrophe. We are permanently in an exceptional state; nay, we are permanently in an unnatural state; this is what is meant by the Fall of Man. Even if we do not admit the Fall of Man, we must admit his continuous state of the staggers. The apple that Eve ate was an orange; and its peel has ever since strewed the ways of the world. As a consequence ... the existence of a proper balance is principally demonstrated, not by people successfully preserving it, but by people swaying hither and thither in their efforts to find it.'†

That is not the language of the divinity schools. But it is sound theology – and anyhow, what would have been the use of talking the language of the divinity schools to readers of *The Bystander*? If Christian belief was to be re-stated in a way that ordinary people could understand and with full awareness of the grounds on

* *Daily News*, September 2nd, 1905.
† *The Bystander*, May 11th, 1904.

54

which it had been attacked, this was the way to begin. There was no Christian doctrine in more urgent need of re-statement than the doctrine of the Fall, because, properly understood, it provided the only alternative to a completely despairing view of the human situation. Chesterton felt this very strongly; and it is interesting to see how often he comes back to it in those early writings of his.

His influence on Christian apologetic has been so great – so much of what he said has been assimilated into the thought of later authors who learnt from him – that it is not easy nowadays to appreciate the originality of his methods and the force of arguments that he was the first to advance. He once observed that –

'There is no nobler fate than to be forgotten as the foe of a forgotten heresy, and no greater success than to become superfluous.'*

And in a measure that fate has been his own. So many fashions of thought that he combated have blown away into oblivion. It is certainly difficult today to realize the sense of renewed hope, of illumination and lifting of the heart that his writings brought to countless Christian people, bewildered and disheartened as they were by the onslaughts of their antagonists and the sense of their own weakness and disunity. Ideas that have become commonplaces of Christian apologetic, arguments that have been used so often as to become platitudes, are found time and again to have been originated by him and by no one else. And until he entered the lists, there was no Christian writer of repute who was capable of such a task.

IV

The particular circumstance that first brought Chesterton into the front line of Christian controversy was the *Clarion* campaign of 1903. *The Clarion* was an extremely well-edited Socialist weekly, directed by one of the ablest journalists of his day, Robert Blatchford. In the later part of 1903 the paper launched a considered attack on the Christian religion. The main ground of the

* Specimen number of *G.K.'s Weekly*, November 8th, 1924.

attack was that the Church was indifferent to social injustice and was no more than the subservient ally of capitalism. When it came to discussing Christian belief, it was very apparent that Blatchford had no idea what historic Christianity really was. The actual object of his strictures was something quite provincial and ephemeral – that same Victorian Calvinism against which the New Theologians were reacting so strongly. Blatchford was more uncompromising, for he simply denounced the whole Christian affair as an imposture which had been exploited to keep the working classes in subjection and terrify them with threats of hell fire if they did not behave.

After the opening phases of the *Clarion* campaign, Blatchford chivalrously threw his columns open to anyone who wished to reply. For three months no member of the *Clarion* staff was allowed in the ring. Then a further series of articles summed up the controversy and drove home its main points.

Much of what Blatchford and his colleagues had said was entirely true and could have been written by a convinced Christian. Indeed, when the embers of the controversy were dying down, Conrad Noel added a decisive last word in the columns of the *Daily News*.

'We must always remember,' he wrote, 'that the main object of rationalist attack is the popular theology of fifty years ago, and not the religion of today nor the religion of the Gospels, nor of the first centuries, nor of what are called the "Dark Ages". . . . Everyone knows of this curious theology and nobody believes it or reckons with it, except the very ignorant and conservative agnostics who still fuss and chatter round it and preach about it and treat it as of the utmost importance. The thinking, living Christian has outgrown it, forgotten it. . . . There is no objection to any Christian reading the works of Messrs Blatchford, McCabe, Robertson and Co., except this: that they will find the religion against which these gentlemen direct their attacks, much more effectively demolished by the leading theologians of the Anglican, Roman and Presbyterian communions.'*

One sequel to the controversy was the publication in the sum-

* *Daily News*, September 23rd, 1904.

mer of 1904 of a sixpenny paper-backed volume entitled *The Religious Doubts of Democracy*. It was edited by a Labour journalist, George Haw, and consisted of a number of the most important contributions to the *Clarion* discussion on the Christian side. Four of the component essays were by Chesterton; other contributors included James Adderley, Charles Marson, Margaret Benson and George Lansbury. One or two of the articles were a good deal above the heads of the kind of reader for whom they were intended; but, by and large, the book was an excellent piece of popular apologetic.

Chesterton's four essays were in his best vein. In her biography Miss Maisie Ward has acutely emphasized their importance and, with great selective skill, has reprinted the most significant passages. Their interest lies in the fact that they are, so to say, first drafts of ideas that were to be expounded five years later in the fuller context of *Orthodoxy*. This is rather specially characteristic of Chesterton; and when people say that he wrote too much and deplore the amount of time he gave to journalism, it is worth reminding them that, time and again, ideas which are fully worked out in what may be called his major works, had first been thrown out and rehearsed in newspaper articles, book reviews and so forth. That was the way in which the final form of his books was hammered out. Thus, his glorious book on St Francis of Assisi was the crown and fulfilment of a whole series of writings – schoolboy verses, the essay in *Twelve Types*, a couple of *Daily News* articles and other appreciations of the saint – written over a long span of years. Some articles that he contributed to *Blackfriars* in 1922–3 contain the rough, preliminary material for some of the most important chapters of *The Everlasting Man*. And it was the same with the *Clarion* articles in relation to *Orthodoxy*.

Half a century has passed since *Orthodoxy* first appeared and it may be that it is not much read at the present time. But in the ten or twenty years following its publication its influence was incalculable. At what may be called the popular level *Orthodoxy* was the pioneer of a completely new approach to the proclamation of Christian truth. It wrested the initiative from the sceptics and presented the historic faith upon a note of triumphant challenge. That in itself was something quite new. The book was a trumpet-call, a *sursum corda*; and it was as exciting as a voyage of discovery.

Orthodoxy is not a theological treatise; Chesterton called it 'a sort of slovenly autobiography'. It is the account of how one man, groping his way through the contemporary fog of negation and half-truth, came out at last into the light of day, believing himself to have discovered some new vision of reality. Only when he had had time to look round and take stock of his surroundings were the facts revealed. What he had discovered, to his own vast astonishment, was the ancient faith of Christendom as handed down by the church in the articles of the Apostles' Creed.

Orthodoxy gathers up the whole of Chesterton's thought to the time when he wrote it and there is not a word in the book that he would have disowned twenty-five years later. It owes something to his own reading – one sees here and there the influence of such writers as Sir Thomas Browne, Blake, Browning and Newman. But in the early chapters Chesterton makes it clear that he had not been drawn towards Christianity by studying Christian apologetics. On the contrary, it was the great agnostics – Huxley, Bradlaugh, Herbert Spencer – who had first unsettled him and sharpened his instinctive protest against the prevalent orthodoxy of agnosticism. It was after reading Colonel Ingersoll's atheistic lectures that the thought broke across his mind, 'Almost thou persuadest me to be a Christian'.

The main argument of the book begins with Chapter IV. It begins where most autobiographies begin, in the nursery. The famous chapter entitled 'The Ethics of Elfland' is the mature expression of thoughts that went back to childhood, and from that point onwards the successive chapters can be fairly closely related to the stages of the author's own development. The chapter called 'The Flag of the World' may be said to cover the unsettled years when he was at the Slade School and starting his first job as a publisher's reader. 'The Paradoxes of Christianity' belongs to the early years at Overstrand Mansions, to his first awareness of what Christian orthodoxy was and to his acceptance of it. In 'The Eternal Revolution', with its passing references to Blatchford and Whistler and Wells and Tolstoy, we have moved on to the period of 'Heretics' and 'Charles Dickens'. The two concluding chapters throw down the challenge of orthodoxy as the only safe guardian of morality, the only sure foundation of freedom, and the single pillar of truth.

An attentive reading of *Orthodoxy* shows the dominance throughout its pages of certain ideas which were in particular need of emphasis at the time when the book was written. Its first concern is to state, in the simplest possible terms, the Christian doctrine of creation – the elementary truth that, in relation to its maker and sovereign, the whole order of created things is contingent and derivative.

Chesterton was fond of saying that his first philosophy was learnt in the nursery, from the fairy tales of Hans Andersen and George Macdonald and from the glorious illusionary world of the toy theatre. They gave him the primary idea of the world as a surprising place, and of human life as something essentially adventurous. In fairyland there are elemental laws that cannot be broken without disaster. There are mysterious ideals of honour and loyalty and obedience and reparation. Fulfilment always hangs upon a veto. Happiness is hedged about by apparently irrational conditions.

'Of all forms of literature, it seems to me,' he had written some years earlier, 'fairy tales give the truest picture of life . . . We learn first and foremost that all doors fly open to courage and hope. We learn that the world is bound together in mysterious bonds of trust and compact and prevision, and that even green dragons keep their promises. We learn that nothing is wasted in the mills of the world, that a jewel thrown into the sea, a kindness to a stricken bird, an idle word to a ragged wayfarer, have in them some terrible value and are here bound up with the destiny of men.'*

This rang true to the facts of experience, but at the same time it was quite inexplicable. Real life, like the fairy stories, was full of things that make you jump with surprise. You could not look at a dandelion or an old cab-horse, you could not listen to the croak of a frog or the hoot of an owl, without a sense of wonder

* Review of Andrew Lang's *Violet Fairy Book* in *The Speaker*, October 12th 1901.

and, in the strict meaning of the word, admiration; and this sense of wonder had a positive element of praise and gratitude which, in turn, could only be satisfied if there were someone (or something) to praise or to be grateful to. It is, anyhow, the exact opposite of that crude arrogance, so characteristic of scientific materialism, which regards the natural world as something that only exists to be conquered or exploited. Against that attitude, which he regarded as nothing short of blasphemous, Chesterton insisted that a certain submissiveness towards the created order and a sense of thankfulness for its existence are essential to a man's understanding of the world he lives in.

The whole affair, of course, was utterly mysterious. Confronted by the universe, you could only wonder why it had been created at all. It seemed on the face of it a most odd thing to have happened; and if you accepted the idea that creation implied a creator, then presumably no one but he could possibly say what it was for. Christianity affirmed that he had not only brought the world into being but had chosen to concern himself actively with its courses, exercising his sovereignty by the operation of laws which could not be disregarded without peril, and by the use of agencies, notably the free will of man, which implied a voluntary limitation of his powers. In contradiction, then, to all forms of pantheism and to the religions of pure immanence, Christianity insisted on the absolute transcendence of God over his creation and, in a carefully guarded sense, his distinctness from it. Chesterton made the point in a characteristic passage.

'All creation is separation. Birth is as solemn a parting as death. It was the prime philosophic principle of Christianity that this divorce in the divine act of making (such as severs the poet from the poem or the mother from the new-born child) was the true description of the act whereby the absolute energy made the world. ... God had written, not so much a poem, but rather a play; a play he had planned as perfect, but which had necessarily been left to human actors and stage-managers, who had since made a great mess of it.'*

Twenty years and more after writing *Orthodoxy* Chesterton

* *Orthodoxy*, pp. 140–1.

came back to this idea and made it the theme of a play called *The Surprise*. It shows a dramatic action played first by puppets who exactly carry out the author's intention, so that his purpose in writing his play and creating his characters is perfectly fulfilled. Yet the author is not satisfied. He is aware that his characters live in his own mind, but not in their own right. They are not separated from him and they have no wills of their own. So, in the second act, the puppets come to life and the same action begins; but this time it is played by living men and women who behave in ordinary human fashion and consequently make havoc of the play. At last the author can stand it no longer.

'In the devil's name,' he cries out suddenly from the wings, 'what do you think you are doing to my play? Drop it! Stop! I am coming down.'

And the final curtain falls.

'I am coming down.' That is the only thing to do. Here is the central Christian paradox – the author invading the stage, the creator visiting his people to reveal his purposes and to dwell amongst them. *Descendit de coelis et incarnatus est.* And it is to be noticed that Chesterton, in writing of Christ, always throws the emphasis upon his manifest divinity. The tendency of contemporary theology had been to stress the gracious humanity of the Saviour, the compassion for the afflicted, the tender love of children, and so forth. There was also a good deal of modernist thought which soft-pedalled the miraculous elements in the gospels and, in its extreme forms, came near to reducing the person of Christ to purely human stature. Against this Chesterton's reaction was wholly salutary and very much needed. In any re-statement of Christian belief there was urgent need to remind men of the Christ of the gospels whom the chief apostle hailed as the son of the living God – of the mighty works and the terrific prophecies, the fierce denunciations, the impossible demands, the majesty and the absolute authority of one who spoke as no man had ever spoken before.

Christianity is a balance, not a compromise. Christ was not, if the term may be used, a compromise between the divine and the human; he was, in Chesterton's phrase, both things at once and both things thoroughly, perfect God and perfect man. This, of course, is plain Christian doctrine. There is nothing original about it. What was original was the manner of its exposition in Chesterton's hands. He made no attempt to come to terms with the various forms of scepticism which were seeking to undermine the foundations of Christian belief. He met the sceptics on their own ground and attacked them with their own weapons of cool reasoning and genial ridicule.

The sceptical attack came from many different angles. Indeed, as Chesterton pointed out, it seemed to be an extraordinary fact about the Christian religion that it could be attacked at one and the same time for precisely contradictory reasons. It could be denounced on the one hand as a thing of gloom and repression and dreary asceticism, and on the other as preaching a fatuous optimism with 'pie in the sky' for everyone at the end of the story. A dozen other examples could be given. You could pretty well match the contrary accusations against one another, so that they cancelled each other out. And what Chesterton brought out more clearly than any other Christian apologist of his time was that, if the Christian revelation was true, it was something absolutely central and unique.

The sceptics, of course, denied that claim and they found considerable support for their denial from the new knowledge in anthropology and from the study of comparative religion – Frazer's *Golden Bough* appeared in 1890 and a revised and enlarged edition came out in 1900. Popular writers such as Mrs Besant and H. G. Wells were pointing out that Christianity and Buddhism were really very much alike. Others were explaining that the Christian eucharist was a mere throw-back to the blood sacrifices found in primitive rites or, again, that the veneration of the Blessed Virgin was simply a Christian adaptation of the worship of Isis. It was an easy game to play if you had read a bit of anthropology and ancient history, and its implications were obvious. It was not difficult to infer that the great religions of the world were all much of a muchness; they might differ in their outward forms and ceremonies, but substantially they all said the same. So far as they did differ, it was mainly in reflecting the characters and needs of the different peoples that had adopted them.

It is, indeed, obvious enough that there are remarkable similarities of one kind and another between the great religions of the world. It is also true that, in St Paul's words, God has never left himself without witness and has in all ages revealed himself in various modes according to men's needs. But Chesterton saw at once that the sceptical writers of his time were not using the facts properly. To say the least, the facts were capable of quite different interpretation. The similarities between religions that had been pointed out were, for the most part, one of two things; they were either without significance or they were similarities from which the wrong conclusions had been drawn.

Thus, it was true that all the great religions teach the virtues of generosity, mercy, self-discipline and so forth. But that is not to say that they are alike in any significant sense; it is merely saying that they are not completely opposed to all human experience. Or again, it was correctly observed that other religions besides Christianity ascribe some form of divinity to their founders. But it was quite irrational to go on to say that therefore all the stories of incarnations are equally legendary or, to put it plainly, equally false.

'The story of a Christ', wrote Chesterton, 'is very common in legend and literature. So is the story of two lovers parted by fate. So is the story of two friends killing each other for a woman. But will it seriously be maintained that because these two stories are common as legends, therefore, no two friends were ever separated by love or no two lovers by circumstance? It is tolerably plain, surely, that these two stories are common because the situation is an intensely probable and human one, because our nature is so built as to make the theme almost inevitable. Thus, when learned sceptics come to me and say "Are you aware that the Kaffirs have a sort of Incarnation?" I should reply, "Speaking as an unlearned person, I don't know. But speaking as a Christian, I should be very much astonished if they hadn't."*

Chesterton did not pretend to write on these matters as an

* *Religious Doubts of Democracy*, p. 18.

expert. He simply claimed the right of the amateur to comment on the facts provided by the specialist; and he showed time and again that the facts were not adequately interpreted by the sceptics and agnostics who were claiming to speak in the name of science.

In the life of Christ the Christian sees the intersection of time and eternity at a definite place and time in history – the godhead made visible, the word of God spoken; God, as it were, putting limits and boundaries to himself so that he could be known to men on their own plane. The Incarnation is the perfect statement of the belief, found in all the great religions, that the spiritual and material are intimately related and cannot be separated. It is not merely that the material symbolizes or suggests the spiritual; it is that each interpenetrates the other. Thus, we find the religious impulse commonly expressing itself in such things as painting, mosaic and statuary to serve the purpose of devotion; in the solemn reading of sacred books; in the use of ceremonial robes and of such material objects as candles, bells or strings of beads as adjuncts to different forms of worship; in the recognition of shrines and holy places as centres of pilgrimage. And in each case there is the underlying idea that the thing or the place is hallowed and in a special sense inhabited by the spiritual reality.

This idea is central to Chesterton's thought. It is the idea that you do not get nearer to the ultimate mysteries by reaching out for the abstract and the infinite. On the contrary, it is always the particular thing that is closest to the thing that passes understanding, the tangible thing that is closest to the spiritual. He says somewhere that a man may be recalled to the visions of his boyhood more vividly by smelling peppermint than by reading about adolescence and that it is possible for Putney to be a more evocative word than Memory. It is the essentially sacramental idea that is found in all the great religions of the world. The most profound mysteries are always related to the performance of a particular action, the journey to a particular place, the use of particular material things. The ultimate realities are not merely symbolized but are actually approached by things as concrete as a house or a loaf of bread or a human voice. Thus, all vision consists in the recovery of that innocence which is the beginning of wisdom and all journeying is ultimately a journey homeward.

'I think', says Innocent Smith, 'that God has given us the love of special places, of a hearth and of a native land, for a good reason. . . . If there be a house for me in heaven, it will either have a green lamp-post and a hedge, or something quite as positive as a green lamp-post and a hedge. I mean that God bade me love one spot and serve it, and do all things however wild in praise of it, so that this one spot might be a witness against all the infinities and sophistries, that Paradise is somewhere and not anywhere, is something and not anything.'*

We have said that one of the main arguments in *Orthodoxy* turns on the point that Christianity is a balance and not a compromise. And if, as Chesterton insists, you are maintaining a balance, you cannot afford to sway or swerve beyond a certain margin of safety. That is what explains the concern of the historic church with the precise definition of its doctrines. Where that was concerned, the church could not afford to swerve by a hair's breadth if the equilibrium of the whole truth was to be preserved; for the Christian revelation is a statement of terrible ideals and earth-shaking doctrines, any one of them powerful enough in isolation to become a false religion and lay waste the world. Therein, as Chesterton saw it, lay the thrilling romance of orthodoxy; and he concludes his exposition with a fine and oft-quoted piece of rhetoric wherein the path of Christendom through the centuries is likened to the equilibrium of a man guiding a team of madly rushing horses, swerving this way and that to avoid the obstacles in his path, yet never losing the mastery of his team or the grace of his balance.

That is a striking simile as applied to the history of the church in the fourth and fifth centuries, and indeed to other periods. The main argument is carried no further. Chesterton had defined orthodoxy as belief in the Apostles' Creed 'as understood by everybody calling himself Christian until a very short time ago and the general historic conduct of those who held such a creed'. That definition, as he was well aware, left a number of loose ends; in

* *Manalive*, pp. 329–30.

particular, it by-passed the question of authority. This was a matter on which, as he acknowledged, he was still in some doubt, and in *Orthodoxy* he deliberately avoided its discussion. He was content to say that he had come to accept the Christian faith on the authority of the church. He had come to recognize the church as the living teacher of revealed truth.

'It not only certainly taught me yesterday, but will almost certainly teach me tomorrow. Once I saw suddenly the meaning of the shape of the cross; some day I may see suddenly the meaning of the shape of the mitre.'*

*   *   *

Chesterton was once asked which he considered his first serious book. He answered '*The Napoleon of Notting Hill*,' and added: 'If I hadn't written it, I should have stopped writing altogether.'

Perhaps it is worth recalling very briefly the main course of the narrative. The action is set in the year 1984. Auberon Quin, the newly elected King of England (whom reviewers were quick to identify with Max Beerbohm) decides in a whim of impish humour to revive the old civic pageantry of the Middle Ages in the modern London suburbs – the ceremonial uniforms, the coats of arms, the battlemented gates to be closed at nightfall, the armed civic guards, the ancient charters and so forth. All this is solemnly inaugurated with much grumbling from local authorities. But in the borough of Notting Hill something unexpected happens. The newly appointed Provost of the borough, Adam Wayne, is a young man who, so far from finding anything absurd or amusing in the King's reforms, takes up his office in a fire of passionate loyalty for the honour and integrity of Notting Hill.

There is a dispute with the borough of Kensington over a scheme of street clearance. Wayne refuses compromise, rallies and arms the men of Notting Hill, declares war on Kensington, and a bitter campaign is fought in the area round Ladbroke Grove and the Portobello Road. There is a decisive battle in Hyde Park and Wayne, facing defeat, retreats on Campden Hill with a remnant of his exhausted army. The combined might of the Kensington

* *Orthodoxy*, p. 285.

forces closes on him; the Provosts of North and South Kensington send heralds to demand surrender.

Then Wayne plays his last card. He retorts that, unless his enemies lay down their arms at once, he will open the Campden Hill reservoir and drown the borough of Kensington in thirty feet of water. To that threat there is no answer. The campaign is over. Kensington surrenders and so the 'empire' of Notting Hill is established.

There follows a period of twenty years of uneasy armistice. At last Kensington, angered beyond endurance by the ever-growing arrogance of the men of Notting Hill, takes up arms again and in the final conflict the power of Notting Hill goes down in ruin.

It is magnificent story-telling, but *The Napoleon of Notting Hill* is essentially an apocalypse, wherein the play of character and the march of events are symbolic of some of the conflicts and paradoxes that lie at the foundations of human experience. Auberon Quin and Adam Wayne, for instance, are well drawn as characters, but they are essentially figures of symbol. They are the two lobes of one man's brain – the two elements in a normal man's make-up which generally exist together in some sort of working harmony, but can fall into a dangerous antagonism when things go wrong. In every man there is both the humorist and the fanatic; the scoffer and the idealist; the misanthropist and the lover; the doubter and the believer. And in a sane way of life they exist together in a healthy tension.

'Auberon Quin,' says Wayne when it is all over and they are talking together in the darkness, 'we have been too long separated; let us go out together. You have a halberd and I a sword; let us start our wanderings over the world. For we are its two essentials.'*

Into the tremendous impetus of the story itself Chesterton put all his most vivid convictions about the society in which he was living – the evil of the great sprawling cities and their shapeless suburbs; the need for wider distribution of property and independent ownership; the unique dignity of the individual man; the indestructible reality of the elemental human loyalties; the place of symbol and ritual in all normal societies; the value and the

* *The Napoleon of Notting Hill*, p. 301.

essential healthiness of the small community. All the fashionable talk of those days about the need for imperialist expansion and economic centralization, for the absorption of the small unit in the greater, for broader views and the blurring of outlines in religion and politics – all this seemed to Chesterton like a doctor prescribing brandy for a man in *delirium tremens*.

'It is precisely from these things that we are suffering,' he had said, ' – from a loose journalism, from a vague geography, from an excitable smattering of everything, from an officious interest in everybody, from a loss of strong national types, of strong religious restraints, of the sense of memory and the fear of God.'*

Chesterton believed that limitation is essential to anything that is to be enjoyed or admired or loved. You must put a wall round Notting Hill if you want people to fall in love with it and be ready to give their lives for it. If you are going to think sensibly about anything, you must mark your limits and define your terms. Chesterton had the sort of mind that rebels against compromise. All his life, as he has told us, he had a particular liking for edges, for the clearly defined boundary, for the sharp rectangle of the picture-frame, for a landscape seen through the clear outline of the arch or window, for the black lines in a drawing which, though they do not exist in nature, separate one object from another – and hence for the sharp distinction and verbal precision of the syllogism. This way of thinking – Aristotelian rather than Platonic, scholastic rather than Augustinian, the vision of Michelangelo rather than Rembrandt – is in a general sense more characteristically Roman Catholic than Anglican. It is certainly true that a man who thinks in these categories and who has been brought up in no particular religious tradition is more likely to find himself at home in the Roman than in the Anglican church.

It is difficult to believe that Chesterton was ever really at home in the Church of England, though he counted himself one of its members for nearly twenty years. He had hosts of Anglican friends and he was always ready to speak on Anglican platforms and to write in Anglican papers. But there seems no evidence for believ-

* 'The Patriotic Idea', in *England a Nation*, edited by Lucien Oldershaw, 1904.

ing that he was ever, in any understandable meaning of the term, a practising churchman. Did he ever go to church on any but the rarest occasions? Did he ever communicate in an Anglican church? Did he ever fulfil the minimum Anglican obligations in regard to the sacraments? As far as we can judge, it would be impossible to give the answer 'yes' to any of these questions.

His biographer was at pains to consult a number of his Anglican friends about this and they were unanimous on one point – Chesterton never went to church. The Rector of Beaconsfield was glad when he became a Roman Catholic, because 'he had always been a very bad Anglican and would presumably become a good Roman Catholic'. Sir Henry Slesser said that Chesterton had a religion of his own and that he never took any part in Anglican worship. Rann Kennedy, an intimate friend from the Battersea days and an Anglican, made the same point with a deeper understanding – Chesterton, he said, 'enjoyed a perpetual eucharist, the eucharist of desire – he was ministered to by angels like our Lord'.*

We are sure that that was true. But it adds emphasis to the belief that Chesterton never seems to have committed himself to the Church of England. This was due partly to his fear, born of a deep and most Christian humility, of being forced into the position of a spokesman or party leader of some kind; it was also due, we think, to the fact that in his heart he was still looking for something that he had not found. Just as he was for a long period a Liberal who did not belong to the Liberal party, so he was for nearly twenty years an Anglican who did not belong to the Church of England.

He was always grateful for the liberal atmosphere of his upbringing and for the fact that he had not inherited, as he put it, either the Protestant faith or the Protestant feud. At no time in his life would he have called himself a Protestant. He had only one reason for remaining an Anglican and that was the belief that the Anglican Church was an authentic part of the one Catholic and Apostolic Church of the creeds, the belief that he was himself a Catholic in virtue of his Anglican baptism and membership. Yet that membership was never more than external. The ordinary Christian of

* Ward, *Return to Chesterton*, pp. 236–7.

whatever denomination is not usually much concerned with religious controversy. He is mainly sustained in his faith by the routine of worship and instruction, the use of the appointed channels of grace, the sense of belonging to a society of a particular character and sharing its life, the observance of its discipline, and so forth; it is in the power of these things that he seeks to live his life as a Christian. As far as we can tell, Chesterton never knew the Anglican church in this way. He was never really within it and, being the great journalist that he was, he tended always to see it with the eye of the journalist and to judge it by what he read about it. He could rejoice in belonging to the same church as Charles Gore and Henry Scott Holland and Philip Waggett; but it was quite another thing to belong to the same church as Dean Inge who wrote every week in the *Evening Standard* and once referred to the Roman Church as 'this bloody and treacherous corporation', or Dr Henson with his robust Erastianism or Dr Major with his extreme modernism – and these were the men who hit the headlines all the time.

The Anglican ethos may not be easy to understand. It is not easy to be an Anglican and it was perhaps less easy fifty years ago than it is today. It can involve almost unbearable tensions in loyalty to an absolutely distinctive ideal. Suffice it to say that the philosophy of Anglicanism is not in general a philosophy of sharp edges, and also that the Church of England is something more than the riot of clerical eccentricity and indiscipline that it commonly appears to be if one only reads the newspapers. It was the comprehensiveness of the Anglican church, using the term in this journalistic sense, that finally persuaded Chesterton that it had no claim to the title of Catholic; and he expressed an ironic gratitude to Dr Inge and Bishop Henson and others for helping him to decide this question.

It seems clear enough that he would have joined the Church of Rome long before he actually did so, if his wife had been ready to accompany him. That was a consideration that weighed heavily with him. It took him, maybe, fifteen years to make his decision and it was the only major decision in his life that he ever made without her. There can be no doubt that he was already uncertain of his Anglican allegiance at the time when *Orthodoxy* was published. When he became so ill in 1914, he asked Fr John O'Connor, if need arose, to give him the last sacraments according to Roman rites. There are many passages in such books as the *Short History of England, The New Jerusalem* and *Irish Impressions* (all written in his nominally Anglican days), which imply an unqualified loyalty to the Roman Catholic Church. It is no accident that MacIan, the Christian spokesman in *The Ball and the Cross*, is a Highland Catholic. And it is no accident that the most persuasive of Chesterton's Christian spokesmen, Father Brown, who made his first bow in 1911, should be a Roman Catholic priest – Father Brown who is, first and foremost, a Christian moralist with a deep and compassionate understanding of human frailty, a severely practical knowledge of the world around him, and a wisdom which most often springs precisely from his profession as a priest. The only Anglican cleric we can remember in the Father Brown cycle is the vicar who murders his brother in the story called 'The Hammer of God'.

Chesterton's reception into the Roman Church was for him a final home-coming. The controversial issues between Rome and Canterbury – the papal claims, Anglican orders and the rest – never seriously exercised him. It is a curious fact about his little book *The Catholic Church and Conversion* – a generous and persuasive essay in apologetics, written with all his old zest and high spirits – that you would not suppose that its author had ever been an Anglican. It is a book that, with very little alteration, he could have written at any time in the previous twenty years. Since he had first become a Christian he had believed every article of the Catholic faith; the whole habit of his thought was Catholic. In a sense, indeed, this had been true long before he became a Christian; there are drawings made in his childhood, essays and poems written when he was a boy at St Paul's, passages in *The Wild Knight* and in his earliest published essays, which show a close sympathy with, and understanding of, the Catholic tradition and way of life.*

---

* One recalls his observation that 'if every human being lived a thousand years, every human being would end up either in utter pessimistic scepticism or in the Catholic religion.' *William Blake*, p. 209.

When he moved into the Roman Catholic Church, there was nothing for him to disown or abandon, and very little for him to add to what he already believed. His conversion was simply the end of a journey, the fulfilment of a pilgrimage, the joining of a family to which he already belonged in all but fact. Once the decisive step was taken, he found that he could continue to expatiate on any aspect of Catholic teaching and belief, all of it already familiar to him, knowing that it was just 'orthodoxy'. The acceptance of the papal authority was for him part of a perfectly logical sequence of thought, for he had always argued from Roman as distinct from Anglican premises. It is probably true to say that he was never an ultra-montane, and some years after his death Belloc went so far as to lament to A. G. Gardiner that 'Gilbert never understood the Church'. In whatever sense this strange remark is to be interpreted, it certainly shows that Belloc never fully understood Chesterton.

*　　*　　*

We have already said something of Chesterton's journalistic work in the post-war period. His *Illustrated London News* essays continued to appear week after week. *The New Witness* died and *G. K.'s Weekly* was born, bringing with it an immense burden of work and responsibility. During the last decade and more of his life he was working harder than ever before. He was in increasing demand as a contributor to the Catholic press and he was writing regularly in at least one American paper. A number of the articles that he wrote for the *Universe*, the *Catholic Herald* and other Catholic journals were collected in two books of essays called *The Thing* and *The Well and the Shallows*. Both contain some good work. A number of the essays, naturally enough, deal with rather narrowly controversial topics, and in a tone calculated rather to entertain the converted than to persuade the outsider. But the two books do contain some first-class apologetics, along with a good deal that shows unmistakable signs of strain and fatigue. One gets to recognize these signs so readily when one really knows Chesterton; and as one reads some of the too facile knocking down of Aunt Sallies or the wearisome attacks on Bishop

Barnes and Dean Inge and Sir Arthur Keith, one seems to catch something of the weariness of the writer himself.

The First World War marked the decisive end of an epoch. Many men who had reached maturity in the pre-1914 years could never fully adjust themselves to the moods and values of the post-war world. They were angered and bewildered by the light-hearted cynicism of the 1920s and the drifting pessimism of the 1930s. They went on writing as well as they had ever written; but their influence was never what it had been prior to the war.

Certainly there was much in the post-war world that Chesterton and other men of his generation detested and deplored, not least the vigorous recrudescence of many abuses and evils which the war effort had held in check. In those first years after the armistice he felt very much as the Ancient Mariner had felt –

> The many men so beautiful
> And they all dead did lie
> And a thousand thousand slimy things
> Lived on; and so did I.

As the years passed, there did come into much of his writing, particularly on social and ethical questions, a note of exasperation and mere scolding. Perhaps it reflected a growing sense of his own isolation, an awareness that he was often speaking in categories which the post-war world hardly understood, let alone believed in. The best of his later books – *St Francis of Assisi, The Everlasting Man* and *St Thomas Aquinas* – and the studies of Cobbett, Stevenson and Chaucer, which also belong to those years, have the common quality that they are all concerned with the past and not the present.

The Everlasting Man is certainly one of Chesterton's most important books. It is in a sense the completion of *Orthodoxy*; or rather, it is the extension and development of the thesis of *Orthodoxy* over the general field of the history of man.

Early in the 1920s a papal encyclical, discussing the mental and spiritual ferments of the post-war years, used the phrase, 'This is an age in which we must defend human dignity'. The words stuck in Chesterton's mind and he turned them like a searchlight on the contemporary scene.

'Let every man', he wrote, 'of sufficient culture to know that every age has its besetting sin, sit down and consider the contradictions of our age. . . . Let him consider what there really is in common between a dance-room full of gigolos and giggling vamps dancing to the latest American jerks and, on the other hand, let us say, a dreary, sullen, sodden German war-book full of filth and despair. Let him consider what is the general spirit that is common to elaborately organized newspaper stunts, blazoning the prospect of Hollywood's brightest star descending by parachute on Brighton pier, and yet also to dim, shady, tottering young men who let women pay for their pleasures. Let him consider what is violated both by endless farces in bedrooms and endless melodramas full of Chinese tortures; let him realize what it is in himself that still revolts against a Utopia of broad grins and ugly advertisements, and also against a bullying biologist who perpetually insists that man is a miserable monkey and that his only end is mud. Let him think of all these things, apparently very different, and then of what they challenge or insult; and I fancy he will find himself repeating with a fresh understanding, "This is an age in which we must defend human dignity".'*

The Everlasting Man is concerned with precisely that task. It is an essay in defence of human dignity. It sets out to re-state the Christian doctrine of man and to illustrate that doctrine by the known facts of history. Almost alone amongst Christian apologists of his time, Chesterton had been grappling with this question since he had first started to write; and in *The Everlasting Man* he divides it into two parts entitled 'The Creature called Man' and 'The Man called Christ'. In the first part, which surveys the human record from its earliest beginnings up to the Incarnation, he is concerned to argue that man, so far from being merely a specially gifted kind of animal, is of a different order of being from the animal creation. In the second part he sets out to show two things – first, that Jesus Christ, so far from being merely one of the great religious founders like Confucius or Zoroaster or

* This passage is guaranteed Chesterton, but having copied it into a commonplace book many years ago and having foolishly failed to record its source, we have been unable to trace it again.

Mahomet, is of a different order of being from other men; and second, that just as man is unique in the order of creation and Christ is unique in the human order, so the historic Catholic Church, which was founded by Christ and lives in time by his life, is unique amongst human institutions. As he remarked in another context, 'There is one church as there is one universe and no wise man will waste his time looking for another'.*

Probably *The Everlasting Man* would not have been written if it had not been for Wells' brilliantly conceived and enormously successful *Outline of History*. Chesterton had admired Wells' book and had written a generous review of it in *The Observer*. It was indeed something of a *tour de force* – excellently proportioned, very accurate in matters of fact, extremely well written and inspired throughout by a vivid historical imagination. Its appeal was tremendous and it sold in cartloads. But it had grave shortcomings. In the long section on human prehistory Wells revived all the half-baked evolutionary theories that had been popularly current in his own youth. Throughout the book ran a bitter anti-Christian bias. There was a hearty contempt for the whole legacy of Rome, pagan as well as Christian. The European middle ages were dismissed in a page or two as sunk in ignorance and superstition, and undeserving of serious notice. The new democratic age of the twentieth century was hailed as the climax of the whole human story and the final herald of the Good Time Coming. It was history for suburbia, made the more plausible by Wells' assumption throughout of a sham impartiality. The book was in fact violently propagandist in purpose; and Belloc's devastating attack on it in his *Companion to Mr Wells' Outline of History*, though too vindictively personal in tone, destroyed its reputation once and for all as a serious historical work.

Many years previously Grant Allen had written a book called *The Evolution of the Idea of God*, which had prompted Chesterton to observe that it would have been much more interesting if God had written a book about the evolution of the idea of Grant Allen. He had added the perfectly fair comment that what Grant

* *Blackfriars*, January, 1923.

Allen really meant by his title was 'I will show you how this non-sensical idea that there is a God first originated among men'. Wells' purpose, no doubt partly unconsciously, was very much the same; but he approached his task, not in a mood of robust denial, but in a sort of glow of emotional agnosticism. This attitude of mind exactly hit off the kind of thing that his public wanted to read. There were all the vague popular notions about evolution – that man 'evolved' from a monkey, that civilized societies have always 'evolved' from barbarism, that the whole business of religion has 'evolved' from the myriad forms, most of them fairly unpleasant, of primitive superstition, and that Christianity was merely one – and by no means the most attractive – amongst the many forms of religion found in the modern world.

'I wish', Chesterton had reflected, 'that there was a real philosophy of comparative religion and one that was not full of inhuman nonsense. . . . A man will say that the feeling about a Madonna is Now I know what a Christian feels about the idea that Michael smiting Satan is the same as that about Mithras who slew a bull. Now I know what a Christian feels about the idea that Michael smote a rebel angel. I do not in the least know what a Mithraist felt about the idea that Mithras killed a bull. It may have been something like the Christian feeling for all I know; it may also have been the worst sort of heathen feeling for all I know. But to have the thing that I do know explained by the thing I don't know is like nonsense out of *Alice in Wonderland*. . . . If [people] were not so anxious to say that the sacrament and the sacrifice were both cannibal orgies (which is nonsense), they might say that they were both sacrifices and had something to do with the philosophy of sacrifice, which is sense. And then, instead of having less respect for the Christians, we might have more respect for the cannibals. If they were not so anxious to compare the Virgin to a heathen goddess, they might possibly compare them both to a human mother and at least get near to something human, if not to something divine.'*

It is very easy to see how the theme of *The Everlasting Man*

* *New Witness*, November 25th, 1921. Reprinted in *The Common Man*, pp. 217-9.

was sparked off in Chesterton's mind by the *Outline of History*. This is no place for a review of the book's contents, and anyhow a mere summary would serve no purpose here. Essentially it is a brilliantly original study in comparative religion. But it is more than that. As its theme is worked out by Chesterton, the book covers in a tremendous sweep of vision the manifold forms in which man's religious impulse has expressed itself through the ages, and seeks to draw out the essential distinctions that alone give meaning to the story as a whole. Wells had certainly attempted to deal with these questions, but he had failed both through prejudice and lack of knowledge. For instance, in dealing with man's prehistory, he started from the old-fashioned assumption that those cults and observances which seemed the most coarse or irrational or repulsive, were necessarily the most primitive; Chesterton had read enough to know of the abundant evidence of a pure form of monotheism, more primitive than any of the superstitious cults and found in every area peopled by the earliest races of man. Again, it was part of Wells' evolutionary thesis that settled and civilized communities had always developed from 'cave-man' conditions; and Chesterton was rightly concerned to emphasize that from the earliest times of which we have any record, primitive and civilized societies are found existing together.

Many people would regard *The Everlasting Man* as Chesterton's masterpiece. It is far more ambitious in its scope than *Orthodoxy*. It is not a well-proportioned book – the first part is too long and the second too short. Some of the rhetorical passages are very much overworked, and there is no doubt that the book as a whole would have benefited by more careful revision – there are some quite obscure passages whose meaning could have been made perfectly clear by a little re-writing. And, as regards the general thesis, Chesterton could have greatly strengthened his case if he had had a better understanding of the special mission of the Jews, of the continuity of the New Israel with the old, of the fact that the revelation fulfilled in Christ began, not at the Incarnation but with the call of Abraham.

Yet *The Everlasting Man* is a remarkable achievement. If there is such a thing as a Christian interpretation of history, this great book does show in firm outline how it is to be discerned. Strangely enough, it has never been recognized at its true worth and one would guess that it is not much known at the present time. Two recent books about Chesterton do not even mention it.

Towards the end of his life Chesterton made his last great discovery, and the result was one of the best and most characteristic books he ever wrote – the study of St Thomas Aquinas which appeared in the *People's Library* in 1933. He already knew a good deal about St Thomas, but he had never had occasion to study him seriously; and there is a sense in which the preparation of his book on the saint was a voyage of discovery, comparable with his discovery of orthodox theology twenty-five years earlier. For when he began to study the *Summa Theologica* carefully, he found himself at once in a familiar country. He found that he knew his way round. He found a vast synthesis of reasoned thought which confirmed and immeasurably enriched his own deepest convictions about the whole human situation. That synthesis was built upon premises that belong, as Chesterton saw it, to what may be called the common sense of the Christian world, and it seemed to him that St Thomas was, first and foremost, the philosopher of the ordinary man. This is not to say that St Thomas is easy to understand; scholasticism is an extremely subtle and complex system of thought, whose proper study demands a long philosophic training. But at the same time it is true that the whole fabric of St Thomas' teaching rests upon, and also supports, the axioms and intuitions which ordinary people accept.

'Since the modern world started in the sixteenth century,' wrote Chesterton, 'nobody's system of philosophy has really corresponded with everybody's sense of reality – to what, if left to themselves, common men would call common sense. Each started with a paradox, a peculiar point of view demanding the sacrifice of what they would call a sane point of view. That is the one thing common to Hobbes and Hegel, to Kant and Bergson, to Berkeley and William James.'*

Chesterton makes this the keynote of his exposition. The structure of the book follows the usual Chesterton formula – that

* *St Thomas Aquinas*, p. 172.

78

is to say, the first hundred pages or so provide an excellent, if somewhat romanticized biographical portrait of the subject, in which are to be found no dates at all, several factual errors, some extremely penetrating and also some very wild historical judgements, and many flashes of Chesterton's extraordinary intuition when he was writing about an historical character. The remainder of the book is devoted to an examination of the leading ideas in St Thomas' philosophy. This was a task which called forth the most brilliant display of Chesterton's greatest gifts, in particular his power of discussing and interpreting abstract philosophical ideas in plain, everyday language and his considerable equipment as a practical theologian. The book was described by the great Thomist scholar, Etienne Gilson, as being beyond possible comparison the best book ever written about St Thomas. That is perhaps somewhat extravagant praise. What is certain is that Chesterton's *St Thomas Aquinas* is an *œuvre de vulgarisation* of surpassing skill and a most persuasive essay in Christian apologetics.

* * *

The difficulty in trying to write anything about Chesterton is that there is so much of him. Any sentence that one writes about him could be expanded into a paragraph; any paragraph into an essay; and any essay into a book. In these introductory notes we have only attempted to touch on one or two aspects of his work and achievement. As prefacing the passages from his journalism which follow, we have been concerned to emphasize the fact that he was a born journalist and that he cannot be understood unless that is kept in view. We have also given weight to his work as a Christian apologist, believing not only that it was in that field that his genius was most fully displayed, but that it is as a Christian apologist that his influence has been greatest and will prove most lasting. Anyone familiar with the developments in Christian thought and expression during the last generation will recognize Chesterton's influence everywhere.

'The prophet and the poet of the man in the street'; 'the protagonist of normal men'; 'a prophet in an age of false prophets';

'the last of the great English men of letters'; 'the last of the Crusaders' – these are some of the epithets that have been applied to him and we might add that he was also the last of the great journalists; there are certainly no journalists of his type nor of his stature left now. During most of his life he was a strangely solitary figure in the world of letters. He founded no new movement of thought – he would have hated to do anything of the kind. He was, in the most exact sense of the word, a reactionary; all his life he fought for the things that are hard and permanent in the world, drawing his strength from the timeless wealth of the Christian tradition.

It is probable, as Mr Frank Swinnerton has suggested, that it will be at least a hundred years before Chesterton's greatness is fully recognized. He was a solitary figure in the literary world. But in the more real world of human relationships it was very different. No man had a greater genius for friendship and none was more beloved by those who knew him. And amongst those who never knew him personally, who knew him only in his writings, there were many who, when they heard of his death, felt that they had lost a friend and mourned him with a sorrow personal and immediate. No one could ever take his place.

The selections from his unpublished work which follow show him in many moods and are concerned mainly with ideas that are central to his philosophy and teaching. They cannot, of course, be read as a connected whole, but we have arranged the passages to show some general sequence of thought running throughout. Where possible, Chesterton's own titles have been used; but this was not possible with many of the shorter passages, and in those cases we have supplied the titles.

A. L. MAYCOCK.

PASSAGES FROM THE UNCOLLECTED WRITINGS OF G. K. CHESTERTON

THE DEBATER

I have always engaged, and always shall engage, in any sort of discussion on the first principles of human existence.

Daily News, July 7th, 1906

*   *   *

HUMOUR AND GRAVITY

There is one very fixed, and I think very false, conception current in human life – the conception that to laugh at a thing is in some strange way to score off it. The literature of blasphemy, for instance, always assumes that when a thing has been shown to be ridiculous, it has in some way been shown to be disgusting or untrue. So far from having been shown to be disgusting, it has not even been shown to be undignified; so far from having been shown to be untrue, it has not even been shown to be improbable. . . . A thing may be too sad to be believed or too wicked to be believed or too good to be believed; but it cannot be too absurd to be believed in this planet of frogs and elephants, of crocodiles and cuttle-fish. The round earth itself is so round that it is impossible to say for certain that it is not standing on its head.

Nor is it true that the fact of a thing being ludicrous impugns its moral value. Many modern writers seem under the persistent impression that a man or a cause, when it becomes laughable, betrays itself and gives inherent signs of failure. If that were so, scarcely one of the causes that have risen and ruled over the world of men would ever have come into any maturity at all. Science and Christianity, Democracy and Imperialism, conceptions and ideals of the most widely divergent character, are all alike in this one fact, that they were all, at the very first glance, absurd . . . And the matter, of course, goes much further than this, for the element of the laughable is not only always potential, but sometimes inevitable and inherent. There is something about heroic postures and heroic words which renders very probable this reaction of derision and entertainment. Have the humorists ever considered what was the meaning of that 'mocking' to which so many martyrs and prophets are described as subject? The tyrants and the populace did not 'mock' the martyr because they had a natural malice against courage or purity. They 'mocked' the hero or the prophet for a very excellent reason: because the hero and the prophet were really funny.

This being so, we are driven to ask ourselves whether this sense of humour, which is so persistently exalted in our day, really deserves the full measure of its encomiums; whether it is really, as is so constantly implied, a test of character, a guide in conduct, an Ithuriel's spear against evil, a standard and a method, a cloud by day and a pillar of fire by night. It has impugned many sanctities; it also has become a sanctity and it is time it was impugned . . .

Of course it is perfectly evident, were we concerned with what is perfectly evident, that a sense of humour has enormous advantages. It gives us delicacy and a secret independence of mind. It makes a man elvishly quick and accurate. But there is one thing to be said against a sense of humour, a thing that has to be said most seriously and most decisively; it does not assist, it rather hinders, the joy of life. The two elements of joy and humour, of exaltation and amusement, are commonly combined in one eudemonistic theory, in one worship of pleasure. But they are in truth vitally antagonistic. If the hedonist asks, 'Where is the glory that was Greece? Where are the gods and priests of delight?', it ought to be easy to answer him. They have vanished at the first whisper of modern humour. It was not the monks nor the saints that slew them; it was the jesters.

This vital kinship between gravity and pleasure is one of those principles which, once they are realized, explain a perpetually increasing mass of facts. To take one man out of a thousand. Whether or no Gladstone was the best or the cleverest or greatest or most statesmanlike of any particular body of men, there can be no doubt as to one supreme fact about him – he was certainly about the happiest man that ever lived. And this was considerably due to the fact that he was not tormented by any very strong sense

of humour. To have splendid talents, to move in a thrilling
theatre of events, to plan vast remedies, to defend them with
dramatic pronouncements, to believe with equal intensity in one's
own capacity and one's own cause, to enjoy clean habits and
heroic health, to live to a pleasant old age in a glow of fame and
personal dignity; this seems an almost legendary life, but this was
his. But laughter would have spoilt it. It is only necessary to make
one remark about Gladstone's great rival. No one who has enjoyed
the wit and laughing wisdom of Disraeli and really understood its
essence, would be surprised to hear that he was an unhappy man.
Let us rather pray for that appalling gravity which marks the happiest of all human creatures, lovers in ecstasy and children at play.

Black and White, April 18th, 1903

*   *   *

An Atheistic Nightmare

In the whole world of things conceivable there is nothing so un-
mercifully hopeless as an infinity of mere facetiousness, a tyrannical nightmare of jesting. All the really popular humorists such as
Sterne and Dickens have really owed their place by the fireside,
not to the fact that they were humorous, but to the fact that they
were serious, that all their jokes were bubbles upon a great sea of
sympathy. Without this assurance, the human soul is more chilled
and homeless in the world of pure humour than in the Arctic
circle. There are few of us who would not prefer to find ourselves
in the deepest of Dante's hells, throttled in the ice among the
traitors, to finding ourselves in a world such as that which is
eternally renewed by the new comic papers, with their men who
care for nothing but dancing girls and their dancing girls who care
for nothing but money. In the circle of the traitors, amid the black
and crushing memories of perjury and oppression, it might be possible to pass a thousand years with the hope that some mellow and
generous memory might awaken for a moment in the heart of one
of the damned. But the world of pure levity is a world by itself;
its bloodless and godless inhabitants have never had any serious
moments, and to a man with any human capacity for joy their faces

are all as strange and cruel as those of invaders from some other planet. To dream of such a world of unremitting and inevitable jest and luxury would be an atheistic nightmare from which a man might with a good deal of relief awake to be hanged.

The Speaker, August 10th, 1901

*   *   *

THE ANATOMY OF THE JOKE

There is nothing comic about a falling tree. There is nothing really funny about a falling star. And there is very little amusement to be got out of a falling thunderbolt, unless it knocks over some carefully selected and suitable person; such as a sociologist proving that he can foresee all future eventualities or an astronomer disproving the existence of thunderbolts.

In short, a falling star is not fantastic, but a falling man is, or can be, fantastic. Why? I do not believe the question can be fully answered, for the same reason that I do believe the current answers are wrong; because it lies deep in the mysterious matter of what did really happen when man received or evolved the mind that sunders him from the beasts and birds. But I will throw out a few vague suggestions about the proper direction of inquiry.

Man himself is a joke in the sense of a paradox. That there is something very extraordinary about his position, and therefore presumably about his past, is the clearest sort of common sense. Alone of all creatures he is not self-sufficient, even while he is supreme.

He dare not sleep in his own skin; he cannot simply put his own food into his own stomach. He has to put the latter first into an oven and cover the former first with external and foreign hair; always sleeping in somebody else's skin. In one sense he is a cripple amongst the creatures; he is at once imperfect and artificial like a monster with two glass eyes and two wooden legs. He is propped upon crutches that are called furniture; he is patched and protected with bandages that are called clothes.

Properly visualized, he is grotesque, not when he sits on a hat, but when he allows a hat to sit on him. Properly understood, he is not so ridiculous when he sits on a hat as when he sits on a chair; for then he is acting like some monstrous sort of crippled quadruped and equipping himself with four wooden legs. Why the lord of creation is a cripple in this queer sense is an open question; but some maintain that it is because he once had a bad fall.

Now this humorous human quality can, as a matter of fact, be much more easily connected with this old idea of a fall of man than with the current and conventional ideas about the evolution of man. To begin with, the explanation, whatever it is, must be something more or less peculiar to man.

Those who have heard the hyena laugh will not admit that his laughter would add much to the mirth of a happy fireside. The fantastic shapes of the other animals are only fantastic as mirrored in the mind of man. In this sense we may say that the camel's hump and the rhinoceros' horn are human secrets and even human possessions; and that we know the pelican and the penguin better than they know themselves.

To all appearance the animal world is unconscious of the grotesque; and considered in the light of mere animal evolution, there is hardly anything grotesque about their innocence.

But let us entertain, merely as a hypothesis and without any reference to doctrinal details or applications, some such supposition as this. That at some time in the unknowable past the creature that has become man received some sort of shock or revelation, by the expansion of his own or the visitation of other psychical forces, whereby he gained a sense of a separate and more divine destiny; that he afterwards lost this direct vision and lived on a lower plane, so that he was haunted with a curious sensation that the accidents of this world are in a sense alien to him, while their very inappropriateness is mixed with some memories of happiness and some hope of recovery. To put it shortly, he is in a sense pleased to be the only creature who is in the wrong place, while all other creatures are in the right one.

It seems to me that the problem of humour presents one primary condition and difficulty which divides it from most others. It seems to me quite clear that the process which ends in a joke necessarily begins with a certain idea of dignity. The dignity is in some way implied beforehand. Beauty or knowledge might conceivably break on a person without previous implications. But incongruity cannot break on him without the pre-existence or pre-supposition of something with which it fails to be congruous. So far as one can see, that pre-supposition is of something erect and, as it were, respectable about the station or stature of humanity.

We think the projection of an elephant's trunk grotesque because it is near enough to being a caricature of a man's nose. We do not think the projection of a precipice grotesque because it is not near enough to imply any comparison with humanity at all.

The more this dark matter is independently considered, the more, I think, we shall find this human standard, as of an erect figure, dominating it like a statue. All depends on this dim or fantastic tracing everywhere of the image of man; and I believe the key is somewhere in that mysterious oracle which identified it with the image of God.

Hearst's International, June, 1922

*   *   *

PUNCH AND JUDY

There is something which is popular and still poor. There is something that is successful and yet bankrupt. There is a drama before the public which the public always applauds. It has run for a million nights and still it does not pay. That is a case for municipal enterprise. I propose that Punch and Judy should be put on the rates.

I have heard the oddest things said about Punch by literary men. I have heard him called Pagan. I have heard him degraded to the level of the Superman. Surely, however, it is obvious that Punch is the most Christian of all possible figures. Punch is Christian because Punch is grotesque.

The one thing that we have all forgotten about Mr Punch is the one thing that our fathers made most prominent – his hump. The victories of Punch are, indeed, the victories of a violent person, but they are the victories of a hunchback. That is, they are the victories of a grotesque cripple. No human being of any imagination ever took the smallest interest in the victories of the strong. It is only the victories of the weak that can be interesting. And all the victories, almost literally without exception, which humanity has celebrated at all, have been the victories of the weak – the weak in size, as in Jack the Giant-killer; or in numbers as at Marathon or Thermopylae; or in station and obvious chances, as in Cinderella or modern socialism; or in bodily defect, as in the blind Samson or the hump-backed Punch.

There are, indeed, human stories like that of Samson, of a man stronger than any other individual man. But there are no stories of this strong man conquering another weaker man and exulting in his strength . . . Strong as he is, his enemy must be stronger than he. And this is obviously the real meaning of Mr Punch. The whole point of the drama is that one highly ridiculous person with a hump is a match for all the organized forces of society, including the Beadle and the Hangman. The emphasis is not on the fact that he claims victory or has a right to expect it; the point is that he does not expect the victory, but does get it. The whole point of the story is that of a forlorn hope. The whole point is not that Punch puts his foot down, but that he has his back to the wall . . .

But the moral claim of Punch and Judy, though obvious, is not its only claim. Artistically it represents something sadder than a lost art; it represents a frustrated art. The technical conception of the whole thing, that of managing a doll with the thumb and two fingers, is exactly one of those direct arts that ought not to be allowed to die. It is probably as subtle as fencing, which is also chiefly managed by the thumb and forefinger. There must be men who can do it, undeservedly starving amongst men who cannot do it. The ragged English Punch and Judy is infinitely superior (on the first principles of art) to the elaborate and civilized Italian system of marionettes. Marionettes are mechanism, like mere trains and telephones. Punch and Judy is manual labour; it is in a strict sense handicraft. The man works this thing – works it by personal and vital gestures – as if he were himself the actor. It is his own right hand that has become to him a separate person. It is his right hand that has lost or has not lost its cunning. It is his right hand that has taught him terrible things. And when he lifts the three fingers that make a doll into a man, he is lifting the same three fingers that all High Pontiffs have lifted in benediction.

If Punch and Judy is permitted to die, there will die with it three things. First, a genuine historic survival of the old Christian farce, in which the clown or fool always had the best of everybody. Secondly, there will die a definite mode of dexterity; one which could be applied to a hundred other hearty pantomimes besides this of Punch and Judy. Thirdly, it will mean the disappearance of a great pleasure of the poor.

Daily News, October 26th, 1907

*   *   *

PUNCH AND JUDY, II

The art of the Punch and Judy show, like the art of the old guilds, is a handicraft. It is that low thing called manual labour, like the work of the sculptor, the violinist and the painter of the Transfiguration. The interest of it lies in the fact that the only instrument really employed is the hand, and the costume of the comic figure is merely a kind of glove. Everything is done with these three fingers, or rather two fingers and a thumb, with which, in fact, all the mightiest or most ingenious works of man have been done. Everything turns on the co-operation of that trinity of digits: the pen, the pencil, the bow of the violin, and even the foil or the sword. In this respect Punch and Judy has a purity and classical simplicity as a form of art, superior even to what is more commonly called the puppet show – the more mechanical system of marionettes that work on wires. And there is this final touch of disgrace in the neglect of it: that while marionettes are mostly a foreign amusement, Punch has become a purely English survival. It is very English, it is really popular, it is within the reach of comparatively poor men. Who can wonder that it is dying out?

Illustrated London News, October 8th, 1921

*   *   *

The Saint and the Dragon

The primary things in the universe, before all letters and all language, are a note of exclamation and a note of interrogation. The very shapes of them are startlingly symbolic; the first straight and simple, the second crooked and looking like a sneer. The note of admiration is Man, erect and wondering, worshipping the wonderful sky. The note of interrogation is the only thinking thing that was with him in Eden from the first. The note of interrogation is the Serpent, curved and at once cowering and insinuating. The first appreciates; the second depreciates. The two have been allegorized and repeated in every bewildering blazon of mythology and heraldry. St George was the note of admiration; he was Adam in armour. The dragon was the note of interrogation gorgeously engraved, like a capital in a Gothic missal. They have come together in many ages with the sound of steel, the straight swords of simplicity and the curved scimitars of scepticism; nor has there been any other battle since the beginning of the world.

Daily News, July 8th, 1905

*   *   *

A Universal Relevance

You cannot evade the issue of God; whether you talk about pigs or the binomial theory, you are still talking about Him. Now if Christianity be ... a fragment of metaphysical nonsense invented by a few people, then, of course, defending it will simply mean talking that metaphysical nonsense over and over again. But if Christianity should happen to be true – that is to say, if its God is the real God of the universe – then defending it may mean talking about anything or everything. Things can be irrelevant to the proposition that Christianity is false, but nothing can be irrelevant to the proposition that Christianity is true. Zulus, gardening, butchers' shops, lunatics asylums, housemaids and the French Revolution – all these things not only may have something to do with the Christian God, but must have something to do with Him if He really lives and reigns.

Daily News, December 12th, 1903

*   *   *

CREEDS AND COBWEBS

People talk nowadays of getting rid of dogmas and all agreeing like brethren. But upon what can they all agree except upon a common dogma? If you agree, you must agree on some statement, if it is only that a cat has four legs. If the dogmas in front of you are false, get rid of them; but do not say that you are getting rid of dogmas. Say that you are getting rid of lies. If the dogmas are true, what can you do but try to get men to agree with them?

Nevertheless there is something deeper behind the rather vague attack on dogma which is widespread in our world. I think what the honest anti-dogmatists really mean about dogma is something like this: it is quite true that when one is talking to simple people such as children or the very poor, one does not repeat theoretic dogmas in their very theoretic form. One does not use frigid and philosophical language. One does not, in short, define the dogma. But let no one suppose that one is any the less dogmatic. For the simple truth is that, instead of defining the dogma, we simply assume the dogma. A mother does not say to her child, 'There is a personal God, the moral and intelligent Governor of the universe'. She says, 'God will be pleased if you are good'. She is quite as dogmatic as a college of theologians. Nay, she is more dogmatic, for it is more dogmatic to assume that a dogma is true than to declare that a dogma is true. But she is certainly simpler and better adapted to looking after babies than a college of theologians would be. And from this fact flows a singular consequence. It does often happen that the more good or innocent a man is, the more he imagines that he is undogmatic. The truth is that, so far from being undogmatic, he believes his dogmas so implicitly that he thinks that they are truisms. . . .

But if there is one thing psychologically certain, it is that men cannot live wholly by instincts, even wholesome instincts. Men must have theories – even to build a wall. It is neither respectful to them, nor dignified in us, that we should always dance round them and implore them to accept our creed. They will find the truth, as we have found it, who deserved it so much less. And the truth is that a man's philosophy of the cosmos is directly concerned in every act of his life. Call theories threads of cotton; still the strain of life is on those threads. Call the metaphysics of free will a mere cob-web; still in the hour of temptation everything will hang on that cob-web. Call the mystical nature of man a mere fancy; the time may come when nothing but that prevents you from shooting a nigger.

Daily News, February 13th, 1906

* * *

A PLEA FOR POPULAR PHILOSOPHY

What modern people want to be made to understand is simply that all argument begins with an assumption; that is, with something that you do not doubt. You can, of course, if you like, doubt the assumption at the beginning of your argument, but in that case you are beginning a different argument with another assumption at the beginning of it. Every argument begins with an infallible dogma, and that infallible dogma can only be disputed by falling back on some other infallible dogma; you can never prove your first statement or it would not be your first. All this is the alphabet of thinking ... And it has this special and positive point about it, that it can be taught in a school, like the other alphabet. Not to start an argument without stating your postulates could be taught in philosophy as it is taught in Euclid, in a common schoolroom with a blackboard. And I think it might be taught in some simple and rational degree even to the young, before they go out into the streets and are delivered over entirely to the logic and philosophy of the *Daily Mail*.

Much of our chaos about religion and doubt arises from this – that our modern sceptics always begin by telling us what they do not believe. But even in a sceptic we want to know first what he does believe. Before arguing, we want to know what we need not argue about. And this confusion is infinitely increased by the fact that all the sceptics of our time are sceptics at different degrees of the dissolution of scepticism. . . .

Now you and I have, I hope, this advantage over all those clever new philosophers, that we happen not to be mad. All of us believe in St Paul's Cathedral; most of us believe in St Paul. But let us clearly realize this fact, that we do believe in a number of things which are part of our existence, but which cannot be demonstrated. Leave religion for the moment wholly out of the question. All sane men, I say, believe firmly and unalterably in a certain number of things which are unproved and unprovable. Let us state them roughly.

(1) Every sane man believes that the world around him and the people in it are real, and not his own delusion or dream. No man starts burning London in the belief that his servant will soon wake him for breakfast. But that I, at any given moment, am not in a dream, is unproved and unprovable. That anything exists except myself is unproved and unprovable.

(2) All sane men believe that this world not only exists, but matters. Every man believes there is a sort of obligation on us to interest ourselves in this vision or panorama of life. He would think a man wrong who said, 'I did not ask for this farce and it bores me. I am aware that an old lady is being murdered downstairs, but I am going to sleep.' That there is any such duty to improve the things we did not make is a thing unproved and unprovable.

(3) All sane men believe that there is such a thing as a self or ego, which is continuous. There is no inch of my brain matter the same as it was ten years ago. But if I have saved a man in battle ten years ago, I am proud; if I have run away, I am ashamed. That there is such a paramount 'I' is unproved and unprovable. But it is more than unproved and unprovable; it is definitely disputed by many metaphysicians.

(4) Lastly, most sane men believe, and all sane men in practice assume, that they have a power of choice and responsibility for action. . . .

Surely it might be possible to establish some plain, dull statement such as the above, to make people see where they stand. And if the youth of the future must not (at present) be taught any religion, it might at least be taught, clearly and firmly, the three or four sanities and certainties of human free thought.

Daily News, June 22nd, 1907

*   *   *

RUBBISH

This title, however true, is not a mere explosion of my literary modesty. It refers, not solely to the article itself, but also to a superb pile of wood, straw, tar, paper and every random substance which is erected in a field just beyond the end of my garden. It is, as you may guess, a Coronation bonfire; but we remote rustics have to write our articles months, so to speak, before the actual Coronation, and the pile is at present unfinished and indeed deficient. I have ransacked house and garden for some time to find rubbish to assist the conflagration; and my eye has suddenly fallen on a pile of fine old quarterlies, works on agnosticism, etc. These I am carrying across to the bonfire. Do not fancy that when I speak of rubbish, I mean only the things that I dislike. I mean a particular kind of vagueness and verbiage which must be cut away and cleared before a man can deal with his real adversaries. I do not call Socialism rubbish; I call it a very powerful, plausible and dangerous drug. I do not call Imperialism rubbish; I call it poison. But I do call 'true Imperialism' rubbish and 'true Socialism' rubbish, for they amount to nothing more than a mild Pharisaism about one's own marvellous merit in loving one's country or being sorry for the poor. Nor would I treat as rubbish anything, however alien or fantastic, which had a positive significance of any sort. I would not throw into my bonfire the Crown of France or the Koran or the Lord's Day Observance Act or the Stuart tartan. I should not see mere rubbish in things that meant something, even if we cannot now decipher what it was, as in obscure and perhaps frightful figures and legends that crumble on Assyrian bas-reliefs in Bloomsbury, or in that ring of rock that stands over Salisbury Plain like stones in the crown of some primordial king of giants. Nor again would I class as rubbish (in this sense) those other examples in which we can decipher the statements and see that they are untrue; as in the case of the Monument in Fish Street or the scientific works of Mr Haeckel.

But I mean things that *never* meant anything; I mean the statesmanlike pronouncements, the wide outlooks and the well-considered conclusions; I mean whole shelves of Hansard and whole stacks of the Higher Thought Review; all the leading articles that oscillate faintly between two unimportant opinions; all the public speakers who are 'far from saying' this or 'the last to say' that; all the servile compromises justified by 'evolution'; all the things that 'every thoughtful man' is supposed to think; all the things 'modern ideas' are supposed somehow or other to involve; all the owlishly stupid 'rebukes' and 'severe comments' uttered by judges and statesmen in utterly artificial wrath against utterly insignificant things; all the streams of sentimentalism poured out when you turn the tap, in defence of the dirtiest convenience or the dullest hack politics; all the consciousness of the solemnity of the responsibility, all the realization of the reality of the tendency; in short, all that grows in that wilderness of pride and folly, where pomposity grows like tall grass and polysyllables crawl about like caterpillars. . . .

But I must break off; because I have to carry all my modern problem novels and books of philosophy and high-class quarterly magazines across to the bonfire beyond the end of my garden.

Daily News, June 24th, 1911

*　　*　　*

No Such Thing

Educational conferences are always interesting for the simple reason that under the title of Education you can discuss anything whatever that comes into your head. This is the main fact which, in spite of all the talk on the subject of education, no one seems to notice in connection with it. The chief thing about the subject of education is that it is not a subject at all. There is no such thing as education. The thing is merely a loose phrase for the passing on to others of whatever truth or virtue we happen to have ourselves. It is typical of our time that the more doubtful we are about the value of philosophy, the more certain we are about the value of education. That is to say, the more doubtful we are about whether we have any truth, the more certain we are (apparently) that we can teach it to children. The smaller our faith in doctrine, the larger is our faith in doctors . . .

Hence, I believe that the whole business of modern education is an immense imposture or convention, an excuse for grown-up people talking about large matters at large. The poor wretches are forbidden in our time to have a proper human religion; that which they ought to discuss in the form of theology they are driven to discuss under the disgusting excuse of education. Talking about serious questions is a pleasure; it is perhaps the greatest mere pleasure known to man. Even devils (as Milton truly perceived) would discuss theology. But in our time it is a secret pleasure; it is enjoyed in dark corners, like a vice.

I need hardly say that the fact that education allows of a man discussing anything is the reason why I have put it first. The actual text which caught my eye and revealed the vagaries and various possibilities of the theme was the report of the Conference of Head Teachers at which Professor Muirhead lectured on Moral Instruction. The phrase Moral Instruction is generally used, of course, with reference to such a programme as that advanced by the Moral Instruction League; it is generally used as signifying the proposal to substitute certain ethical lessons for the religious instruction (somewhat dim and dubious as it is) which is given in most schools. So far as this meaning is concerned, my own position is a simple and, I hope, an inoffensive one. I even offer a compromise or bargain, exactly as if I were a politician. I am quite prepared to promise the secularists secular education if they on their side will promise (on the tombs of their mothers) not to have moral instruction. Secular education seems to me intellectually clean and comprehensible. Moral instruction seems to me unclean, intolerable; I would destroy it with fire. Teaching the Old Testament by itself means teaching ancient Hebrew ethics which are simple, barbaric, rudimentary, and, to a Christian, unsatisfying. Teaching moral instruction means teaching modern London, Birmingham and Boston ethics which are not barbaric and rudimentary, but are corrupt, hysterical and crawling with worms and which are, to a Christian, not unsatisfying but detestable. The old Jew who says you must fight only for your tribe is inadequate; but the modern prig who says you must never fight for anything is substantially and specifically immoral. I know quite well, of course, that the non-religious ethics suggested for modern schools do not verbally assert these things; they only talk about peaceful reform, true Christianity and the importance of Count Tolstoy. It is all a matter of tone and implication; but then so is all teaching. Education is implication. It is not the things you say which children respect; when you say things, they very commonly laugh and do the opposite. It is the things you assume that really sink into them. It is the things you forget even to teach that they learn . . .

Churches, philosophies, sects, social influences, all educational authorities have disagreed, have distorted each other's meaning, have destroyed each other's proposals, in this matter of education. But here I hope I offer a peaceful proposition on which all churches and all philosophies can agree. I am the bearer of the only real olive-branch. All educational authorities can agree upon the simple proposition that I lay down. There is no such thing as education. Education does not exist. That will indeed be a blessed gospel to spread through the modern world and even my feet will be beautiful upon the mountains when I proclaim it. For indeed this is the nearest statement of the truth. There is no education apart from some particular kind of education. There is no education that is not sectarian education.

Illustrated London News, January 12th, 1907

* * *

THE PROTECTION OF THE BIBLE

It is a matter of great gratification that an official voice in practical education has spoken in favour of that exclusion of all theologies from the national schools for which many have long pleaded. It is a policy promoted, generally speaking, by the most lucid and magnanimous of all parties. Some, and I am one of them, do not wish theology to interfere with education. Some, and I am again one of them, have the greatest horror of education presuming to interfere with theology, which is so much more living and exciting a subject. And a very interesting question is undoubtedly raised by the distinction between the teaching of theology and the teaching of the Bible. The question of whether the Bible can be taught merely as literature is a question that raises the whole riddle of things that have two meanings, a big meaning and a small meaning. Can the Koran be treated as literature? Yes, anywhere except in Islam. Can the Bible be taught as pure literature? Yes, anywhere except in a Protestant country.

There are several popular misconceptions about this educational aspect of Scripture. One quite curious mistake is this. It is always somehow assumed that, if the Bible is taken out of the schools, it will be taken out in the interest of those who do not believe in it. This is a complete mistake. Those who do not believe in it are exactly the people who have no reason to object to it. It is the people who do believe in it who have a right to get restless. A reasonable Freethinker need not have the faintest objection to his child learning a chapter of Isaiah merely as literature. In so far as he is reasonable, he will agree that it is literature, and in so far as he is a Freethinker he will agree that it is only literature. The man who is hardly used by such teaching of the Bible is precisely the orthodox man, the man to whom Isaiah means first and foremost the blood-stirring prophecy of a world-shattering event. I should not mind my children learning Icelandic folklore. Nor should I mind them learning Jewish folklore – if it is only folklore. I should not mind my children being told about Mahomet, because I am not a Mohammedan. If I were a Mohammedan, I should very much want to know what they were told about him.

Therefore I sympathize with secular education, but not because my sympathy is with the new-fashioned Puritan who wishes the Bible to be treated as literature. My sympathy is with the old-fashioned Puritan who does not want the Bible to be treated as literature, because he happens to have a religion which is about the most interesting thing a man can have. It is the old-fashioned theologians who ought to insist on secular education. It is the orthodox Puritans who ought to want the Bible kept out of the schools. The truth can, indeed, be put in a kind of dilemma. Either the Bible must be offered as something extraordinary or as something ordinary. If it is offered as something extraordinary, that is certainly unfair to the agnostics and the doubters. If it is offered as something ordinary, that is grossly and atrociously unfair to the theologians and the believers. ... The Bible compromise is false both to the civic idea of liberty and to the Protestant idea of the Bible.

Daily News, April 17th, 1909

*　　*　　*

SPIRITUALISM

We are told today that we should be better for a religion without a theology. I believe our brains would be the better even for a theology without a religion.

The special mark of the modern world is not that it is sceptical, but that it is dogmatic without knowing it. It says, in mockery of old devotees, that they believed without knowing *why* they believed. But the moderns believe without knowing *what* they believe – and without even knowing that they do believe it. Their freedom consists in first freely assuming a creed, and then freely forgetting that they are assuming it. In short, they always have an unconscious dogma; and an unconscious dogma is the definition of a prejudice. ...

The debate on the ethics of Spiritualism is a strong example of this. The Spiritualists act upon a dogma, which they cannot state dogmatically; and therefore only assume dogmatically. Most Anti-Spiritualists also, I may add, assume a dogma without knowing it – and a much staler and stupider dogma at that. But the point here is that they differ from the old creeds in never being stated clearly as creeds. What a Spiritualist assumes is practically this; it is not

merely the existence of spirits, but the non-existence of evil spirits
– or at least of the extreme evil done to us by evil spirits. To put
it popularly, Spiritualists are optimists about the spiritual world.
The Puritans and the people of the seventeenth century generally
were pessimists about the spiritual world. They thought it a thousand to one that anybody dealing with spirits was dealing with bad
spirits. Hence, they turned even the worst sort of witch-burning
from murder to massacre. These were very appalling deductions
from one axiom – that human nature is nearer to wicked spirits
than to good ones. But at least the Puritans could state their pessimistic axiom as an axiom. The Spiritualists cannot state their
optimistic axiom as an axiom at all; they do not even know it is
optimistic. They simply feel it unconsciously as the spirit of their
time – that is, as something not even as solid as climate, but rather
as fickle as the weather.

Now the main objection to Spiritualism is almost identical with
the claim of Spiritualism. The objection is that it puts a man
under the control of spiritual forces, or that it brings him in contact with the unknown. In fact, it is almost impossible to find any
commendation of such a belief in spirits which will not serve as a
condemnation in the mouth of those who believe in bad spirits.
The very words 'medium' or 'control' will indeed affect many
of us as immoral words – I might say, indecent words. They imply a spiritual surrender which is dubious even if the influence be
good, and shocking if it be bad. Now it certainly is not self-
evident, from the analogy of all we know, that it cannot be bad. . . .
That the investigators do not insist on this danger, or do not insist
on it as dangerous, is simply due to that forgotten first principle to
which I have referred. The Spiritualists are forbidden to accept
the deduction from the Spiritualist parallel because it would involve a denial of the spiritualist dogma. And it is none the
less felt as an infallible dogma because it is an unconscious
dogma. . . . If a man's view of the universe allows him to be the
medium of he knows not what and under the control of he knows
not whom, let him say so and state his view of the universe
clearly, like his fathers before him. Then at least he will not fall
into a mere slush of likes and dislikes, and choose to fancy

angels only with white wings because he prefers them to black ones.

Illustrated London News, March 15th, 1919

* * *

THE ENGLISHMAN'S RELIGION

... that queer, beautiful, laughable thing, the English religious feeling, so hazy, so reverent, so illogical, so humane, so kindly, so vulgar.

The Bystander, June 1st, 1904

* * *

THE ENGLISH WAY

No one can understand the nature of England or of English politics who does not realize that this island of ours is and always has been covered with a kind of beautiful cloud. No one can be a good critic of England who does not understand fogs. And no one can be a really patriotic Englishman who does not like fogs. Of all national histories, the history of England must be the hardest to write, for the English, with all their great epochs, not only did not know what they were doing, but, so far as one can make out, did not want to know what they were doing. They always did a thing in such a way that a hundred years afterwards it could be maintained that they had done the precise opposite. They always said a thing in such a way that it could mean something different. This was not craft . . . It was their ingrained poetry.

There are no people so poetical as the English, no people that are so full of a sense of vague distances and perspectives; there are no people so full of a certain fine formless sentiment. They see all things melting into one another like the mists of their northern sky; the Latin sees everything as clear cut as the crests of the Alps against the hard blue enamel of heaven. The English law, for instance, is uncommonly like an impressionist picture of a rainy day. The Code Napoleon is like a coloured photograph of Rome.

The haphazard, hand-to-mouth quality both in our legislation and our judicature is partly, no doubt, the result of selfish aristocratic raids and intrigues, but is still more the result of a certain dim kindliness, a sort of desperate kindliness, living in the heart of a confusion and never daring to trust itself to a general rule. This quality of a humane vagueness has made inexpressibly difficult the study of all the great European crises in their particular effect on England. It is grasped that what was in other countries a revolution was in England commonly a compromise. But in England commonly it was more than a compromise; it was a riddle. The Reformation came, for instance. Scotland went Protestant; Ireland went Catholic; England went something or other, but what no modern historian can perfectly demonstrate. Englishmen argued with each other, burnt each other, set up and pulled down kings, but all in such a manner as to leave it reasonably doubtful in the twentieth century whether anything happened at all. ... There is something wholly English and quite unexplainable about this innocent juggling; this calm and beneficent humbug.

Daily News, March 16th, 1905

*   *   *

HIGH OR LOW?

The one thing that the modern English will not understand is that when you have lost your way quite hopelessly, the quickest thing is to go back along the road you know to the place from which you started. You may call it reaction, you may call it repetition, you may call it tiresome theory, but it is the quickest way out of the wood. No Ritual Commissions and no other kind of Commissions ever do the least good, because they will not step back to the first facts of the situation. Now the first facts are never material facts. The invisible always comes before the visible, the immaterial before the material, even in our everyday experience ... The modern English will never settle their problems until they understand that the shortest cut to the practical is through the theoretical; and there could not possibly be a stronger instance of it than the instance of ritualism and the Ritual Commission.

The whole point of the quarrel about ritualism is very simple; it is that it is not a quarrel about ritualism at all. Nobody can quarrel about ritualism. If a gentleman, instead of offering me his hand, offers me his foot, explaining at the same time that to him this rite has the same meaning as hand-shaking, I may regard him as amusing, but certainly not as wicked. But if I am offended at such an act, it is because the sudden waving of his foot in the air does not immediately convey its meaning, but may even be regarded by the over-sensitive as a sort of symbolic or non-effective kick. In the same way, nobody cares one atom what any clergyman does in his church. . . . All that any of them care is what a clergyman means. He might have, not two but two hundred candles on the altar if the altar did not mean something – that is if the altar were not an altar. The clergyman might wear six copes and seven mitres if he were wearing them merely as his private taste in the matter of a suit of clothes. In a word, ritual is not even ritual without the question of doctrine. And doctrine, I believe, the Commission was not allowed to discuss.

The ultimate problem about the Church of England is not easy to settle, but it is easy enough to state, and these Commissions have never even heard it stated. It is that a quarrel exists in the Church of England very unique in human institutions. The Church of England is quarrelling about what the Church of England is. The House of Commons is quarrelling about what the House of Commons shall do. The House of Lords is quarrelling about what the House of Lords shall do. Even a private ship quarrels about what it shall do; it does not quarrel about whether it is a private ship or a missionary boat or a man of war. Even a band of robbers quarrels about what it shall do; it does not quarrel about whether it is an omnibus company or a plumbers' union. But the quarrel in the Church of England is not about what it shall do; it is about what it shall be – indeed, about what it has been. Does its whole authority lie in being a branch of the Catholic Church? Or does its whole authority lie in being a protest, a part of the great sixteenth-century protest, against that Catholic Church? All commissions are useless which attempt to discuss what it does, without discussing what it is. Until this first question is settled, it is as childish to discuss a clergyman's vestments as to discuss his wall-paper.

Illustrated London News, July 14th, 1906

*   *   *

STRAIGHT THINKING

Logic and truth, as a matter of fact, have very little to do with each other. Logic is concerned merely with the fidelity and accuracy with which a certain process is performed, a process which can be performed with any materials, with any assumption. You can be as logical about griffins and basilisks as about sheep and pigs. On the assumption that a man has two ears, it is good logic that three men have six ears, but on the assumption that a man has four ears, it is equally good logic that three men have twelve. And the power of seeing how many ears the average man, as a fact, possesses, the power of counting a gentleman's ears accurately and without mathematical confusion, is not a logical thing but a primary and direct experience, like a physical sense, like a religious vision. The power of counting ears may be limited by a blow on the head; it may be disturbed and even augmented by two bottles of champagne; but it cannot be affected by argument. Logic has again and again been expended, and expended most brilliantly and effectively, on things that do not exist at all. There is far more logic, more sustained consistency of the mind, in the science of heraldry than in the science of biology. . . . There is more logic in *Alice in Wonderland* than in the Statute Book or the Blue Books. The relations of logic to truth depend, then, not upon its perfection as logic, but upon certain pre-logical faculties and certain pre-logical discoveries, upon the possession of those faculties, upon the power of making those discoveries. If a man starts with certain assumptions, he may be a good logician and a good citizen, a wise man, a successful figure. If he starts with certain other assumptions, he may be an equally good logician and a bankrupt, a criminal, a raving lunatic. Logic, then, is not necessarily an instrument for finding truth; on the contrary, truth is necessarily an instrument for using logic – for using it, that is, for the discovery of further truth and for the profit of humanity. Briefly, you can only find truth with logic if you have already found truth without it.

Daily News, February 25th, 1905

*　　*　　*

A MAN OF DISTINCTION

It is obvious that there fell with Arthur Balfour one of the few remaining pillars of that old patriotic aristocracy which not only governed England but practically was England, so far as England was a personality dealing personally with other nations. It is one of the paradoxes, so typical of England, that many of the men who thus understood and summed up her policy came from Scotland. It has been said that it requires a surgical operation to get a joke into the head of a Scotsman. I wonder no Scotsman has retorted, what would often be more correct, that it requires a surgical operation to get a serious idea into the head of an Englishman. When it happened, the operation was often performed by a Scotch surgeon. The English squire was an unconscious aristocrat; the Scotch laird was a conscious aristocrat; and Lord Balfour, with all his social grace and graciousness, was conscious and even self-conscious. But this was only another way of saying that he had a mind which mirrored everything, including himself and that, whatever else he did, he did not act blindly or in the dark. He was sometimes quite wrong; but his errors were purely patriotic, both in the narrow sense of nationalism and in the larger sense of loyalty and disinterestedness. ... He was a man of strong and stoical character and nothing showed the falsity of political journalism so much as the legend which represented him as a drooping aesthete or a broken lily. In some ways he seems to me to have been too good a Stoic to be entirely a good Christian; or rather (to put it more correctly) to feel, like the rest of us, that he was a bad Christian. But about his virtues, both public and private, there can be no doubt, for they contained great elements that stood out as rather unique in his time. Courage, dignity, self-control, these were much more the essentials of his character than the social elegance and suavity attributed to him by all his critics and some of his admirers. There was much more in him of the Scotch Puritan than of the English Cavalier.

But he made one great contribution to modern politics which it will be well to understand because it was entirely misunderstood. It is supremely characteristic of the present Parliamentary atmosphere that everybody accused Lord Balfour of incomprehensible compromise and vagueness because he was completely logical and absolutely clear. Clarity does look like a cloud of confusion to people whose minds live in confusion twice confounded. What is called the modern mind is soaked in associations and cannot understand distinctions, even when they are absolutely reasonable distinctions. The people stuffed with our journalese culture or popular science can only understand anything in relation to 'all that sort of thing'; they cannot comprehend that something a little like it is really quite a different sort of thing. . . . They can understand, to take an instance, the general tendency to put more and more things under the control of the State and the argument which says that as the highroad is public, so the railroad should be public; and if the railroad, then the house and the kitchen garden and the cat and the dog must all be owned by the public. They can understand, and perhaps more sympathetically, the contrary process of distrusting the State and putting things back into private hands; first the railroad and then the road and then, for all I know, the Post Office and the Army and Navy. They are acquainted with the sort of expanding cant that can be used at any stage of either of these drifts or tendencies. But if you try to point out what the wisest sages and legislators have meant by the difference between public and private property, if you explain that nationalizing the roads is not the same as nationalizing the land, you will generally find that they are merely puzzled and suppose it to be some sort of mystification – because it is quite clear. They cannot make out whether you are in favour of 'Socialism and all that sort of thing'. Lord Balfour once rent the murky sky of politics with one lightning-flash of lucidity by giving the exact economic definition of the collectivist idea, and then adding, 'That is Socialism and nothing else is Socialism'. It was probably regarded as one of his fine-spun evasions.

That is the intellectual virtue of which Lord Balfour really left a valuable example. People said his distinctions were fine distinctions, and so they were; very fine indeed. A fine distinction is like a fine painting or a fine poem or anything else fine; a triumph of the human mind. In these days when large-mindedness is supposed to consist of confusing everything with everything else, of saying that man is the same as woman and religion the same as irreligion, and the unnatural as good as the natural and all the rest of it, it is well to keep high in the mind the great power of distinction; by which man becomes in the true sense distinguished.

G. K.'s Weekly, March 29th, 1930

*   *   *

St Pius X

Among the many true and touching expressions of respect for the tragedy of the Vatican, most have commented on the fact that the late Pope was by birth a peasant. Yet few or none, I think, traced that truth to its most interesting and even tremendous conclusion. For the truth is that the Papacy is practically the only authority in modern Europe in which it could have happened. It is the oldest, immeasurably the oldest, throne in Europe; and it is the only one that a peasant could climb. In semi-Asiatic States there are doubtless raids and usurpations. But these are of brigands rather than peasants; I speak of the pure peasant advanced for pure merit. This is the only real elective monarchy left in the world; and any peasant can still be elected to it. . . . Even in high and heroic republics like those of France and of Switzerland, can one say that the ruler is really the plain man in power?

Now all the evidence, from foes as much as friends, attests that this really was true of the great priest who lately gave back to God the most tremendous power in the world. Those who admired him most, admired the simplicity and sanity of a peasant. Those who murmured against him most, complained of the obstinacy and reluctance of a peasant. But for that very reason it was clear that the oldest representative institution in Europe was working; when all the new ones have broken down. It is still possible to get the strong, patient, humorous type that keeps cheerfulness and charity alive among millions, alive and supreme in an official institution.

As has been pointed out, with subtle power and all proper delicacy, in numberless liberal and large-minded journals, the great and good priest now dead had all the prejudices of a peasant. He had a prejudice to the effect that the mystical word 'Yes' should be distinguished from the equally unfathomable expression 'No' . . . The Pope never pretended to have an extraordinary intellect; but he professed to be right – and he was. All honest atheists, all honest Calvinists, all honest men who mean anything or believe anything or deny anything, will have reason to thank their stars (a heathen habit) for the peasant in that high place. He left people to agree with his creed or disagree with it; but not free to misrepresent it. It was exactly what any peasant taken from any of our hills and plains would have said. But there was something more in him that would not have been in the ordinary peasant. For all this time he had wept for our tears; and he broke his heart for our bloodshed.

Illustrated London News, August 29th, 1914

*   *   *

THE BLACK LINES

There are about as many definitions of man as there are men. Let me, however, offer the reader another. Man is a creature who creates cataclysms. Man's whole nature and object on the earth is to draw those black lines that do not exist in inorganic nature. He separates things and makes them special. Take, for the sake of an instance, the admirable and fascinating subject of meals. A cow eats all day; its hunger, I suppose, grows gradually and vaguely at the beginning, is slowly and increasingly satisfied, and then gradually and vaguely dies away. It is an evolutionist. But man is made for revolutions, or rather he makes them; he is formed for abrupt departures and great experiments. He faces the cataclysm called

Lunch. It is a thing of black lines; decisive like a religion or a rebellion. It begins at some time and (except in extreme cases) ends at some time. Man makes monogamy, patriotism, oaths before magistrates, monetary obligations, religion, honour, civic obedience, theology, all on the same sacred principle on which he makes lunch. He has less, perhaps, and the cow has more. But then he has something; and the cow only has anything. If man were to run about on all fours eating a field full of mutton chops, his meals would not have the meaning they have now, a meaning of hospitality, comradeship, human symbolism. His mutton chops would not be the mystical things that they are at present. Man is the animal that draws black lines. Sometimes they are lines round a land, and they make patriotism. Sometimes they are lines round an animal, and they make humanity. But in all cases this is true, that men learn to love their limitations, that men learn to love not only the picture, but the frame. Thus artists grow fond of the fact that they are working in wood only, or in iron only, or what not; they love the thing that isolates them. And so those who began by loving England came to love her frame, the sea.

Daily News, September 9th, 1905

*   *   *

THE COSMIC STEW-POT

There has crept into our thoughts, through a thousand small openings, a curious and unnatural idea. I mean the idea that unity is itself a good thing; that there is something high and spiritual about things being blended and absorbed into each other. That all rivers should run into one river, that all vegetables should go into one pot – that is spoken of as the last and best fulfilment of being. Boys are to be 'at one' with girls; ... all sects are to be 'at one' in the New Theology; beasts fade into men and men fade into God; union in itself is a noble thing. Now union in it self is not a noble thing. Love is a noble thing; but love is not union. Nay, it is rather a vivid sense of separation and identity. Maudlin, inferior love poetry does, indeed, talk of lovers being 'one soul' just as maudlin, inferior religious poetry talks of being lost in God; but the best poetry does not. When Dante meets Beatrice, he feels his distance from her, not his proximity; and all the greatest saints have felt their lowness, not their highness, in the moment of ecstasy. And what is true of these grave and heroic matters (I do not say, of course, that saints and lovers have never used the language of union too, true enough in its own place and proper limitation of meaning) – what is true of these is equally true of all the lighter and less essential forms of appreciation or surprise. Division and variety are essential to praise; division and variety *are* what is right with the world. There is nothing specially right about mere contact and coalescence. . . .

In short, this vast, vague idea of unity is the one 'reactionary' thing in the world. It is perhaps the only connection in which that foolish word 'reactionary' can be used with significance and truth. For this blending of men and women, nations and nations, is truly a return to the chaos and unconsciousness that were before the world was made. There is, of course, another kind of unity of which I do not speak here: unity in the possession of truth and the perception of the need for these varieties. But the varieties themselves; the reflection of man and woman in each other, as in two distinct mirrors; the wonder of man at nature as a strange thing at once above and below him; the quaint and solitary kingdom of childhood; the local affections and the colour of certain landscapes – these actually are the things that are the grace and honour of the earth; these are the things that make life worth living and the whole framework of things well worthy to be sustained. And the best thing remains; that this view, whether conscious or not, always has been and still is the view of the living and labouring millions. While a few prigs on platforms are talking about 'oneness' and absorption in 'The All', the folk that dwell in all the valleys of this ancient earth are renewing the varieties for ever. With them a woman is loved for being unmanly, and a man loved for being unwomanly. With them the church and the home are both beautiful, because they are both different; with them fields are personal and flags are sacred; they are the virtue of existence, for they are not mankind but man.

T. P.'s Weekly, Christmas Number, 1910

* * *

The Sentinel

The great conception which lay at the back of the Hebrew and Christian scriptures was the conception that to man had been given a certain law, to champion which was his sole and simple business. 'He hath shown thee, O man, that which is good' is perhaps of all earthly sayings the one which has the deepest ring; it seems, as it were, too true and simple to be comprehended. The stars in their courses might fight against his honour, scientific discoveries might make the world seem more perilous and equivocal; at the turning of a stone or the splitting of a sea beast, the whole cosmic army might seem suddenly to desert to the devil. But man had in his heart a secret which would outlast these things; he had his orders; he was the sentinel of God.

The Speaker, October 19th, 1901

*   *   *

Everyman

The meanest man is immortal and the mightiest movement is temporal, not to say temporary.

Blackfriars, January, 1923

*   *   *

Death of an Artist

The first impulse of any serious person on hearing that G. F. Watts is dead must of necessity be an impulse to say, as we said of Gladstone, 'All the great are dying'. This is not mere journalese. It is a genuine impression and in one sense it is true: there are none left who carry themselves as these great men did. But there is a danger in this mode of speech, and also an error, for in it is involved the very evil of this age, out of which its littleness comes. There are many evils in this particular period of ours. One of the worst, doubtless, is that we never produce great men; but the worst of all is that we are always looking for them. The men of the great time of Watts did not look for great men, but for great causes; and in a great cause almost anyone may become great.

There are none left who carry themselves as these heroes did, because there are none left who are so indifferent to mere intellectual eminence. Watts and such men as he were the children of the great republican revolution that began the nineteenth century, which filled men with a furious belief in humanity and was the latest of the religions of mankind. They were great men because they did not believe in great men; they believed in men. They mingled in a common and equal competition of enthusiasm for something outside individual men, and out of that only comes real individuality. They sought first the Kingdom of God and His righteousness; they sought first the important things, and trifles – such as greatness and genius – were added unto them.

We shall not again have a man of the greatness of Watts until we have something better to think about than greatness. One thing at any rate stands out of his whole character; one thing must be burningly vivid to anybody who ever had, even as briefly as I had, the honour of meeting him; that he himself cared for the thing called greatness not a single straw. He cared only for the spread of certain conceptions, true or false, with which he had identified himself . . . He belonged in this matter, beyond question, to an age of causes and will therefore be found in this matter incredible. If our civilization pursues its present course (which is absurd), he will become in a very short time a heroic myth.

The note of this greatness of his was well expressed in his artistic work, especially his artistic work in early years. Sometimes his work was admirable, sometimes bad, but it was always simple and it was always ambitious. The technique of art is so far from being immoral that a moral transition can be quite easily deduced from it; moral changes can be seen physically in chalk and oil. And one great fact is this: that all the great men younger than Watts sought to work in a style and scheme that was of its nature transient. They wished to decorate a room with peacocks, for rooms are tired of and taken down, or to fill a paper with epigrams, for epigrams are repeated nine hundred and ninety times and then forgotten, or to effect exquisite sketches on brown paper, for these owe their very charm to the fact that they can be thrown away like brown paper. But Watts had the old dream of building in eternal brass; he loved designing public frescoes, public statues, public mosaics. There is a mosaic of his in the Whitechapel Road, a fresco in the House of Lords, a picture in St Paul's Cathedral. One cannot move St Paul's Cathedral as one moves the Peacock Room. One cannot throw away the Whitechapel Road as one throws away brown paper. I am not saying that this monumental solidity proves that the art is great. But I say that it proves that the artist is confident.

Another quality very characteristic of the atmosphere to which Watts belonged is the quality of his moral indignation. He always had the temper of the meliorist, whilst he had at the same time much of the temper of the old Rousseauist optimist. He was really angry with the evils of the modern world. . . . In all his moral and religious allegories, especially when they touch upon the diabolic side of things, there is apparent this sudden and sacred impatience. Under the picture of 'Mammon', under the picture of 'The Minotaur', under the picture of anything evil in his gallery, seems printed in letters of fire 'Shall this be endured for another moment?' And it was this innocent and startled wrath which was the note of the whole of Watts' age, the age of the Reform Bill. It was because the old political idealists had something of the child's ignorance and horror of evil that they swept away so many abuses. Compare with some picture by Watts, which is full of a young and wide-eyed anger, some ultra-modern picture of an evil thing, some work of the new pessimistic atmosphere. Take, for instance, Degas' brilliant picture called 'Absinthe', which depicts two wrecks of humanity soaking themselves in the maddening wormwood. The picture is steeped in devilish resignation. We feel as we look at it that these two human creatures have drunk absinthe from the beginning of the world and will go on drinking it while the grass grows and until the stars fall into ruin. Here there is no astonishment, therefore there is no indignation. There is a thing that may truly be called religious resignation. But there is a deeper and stiller and more terrible thing and its name is irreligious resignation. Because of Watts' intensely religious nature the painting of such a picture as this would be absolutely impossible to him. If he had conceived and painted 'Absinthe', there would have been something fierce and insistent about the picture. Something fiendish and strained in the faces would have declared that the situation was unnatural. Something bitter and burning in the green colour of that shameful wine would have shown like the green eyes of a witch's cat. However dark and repulsive and merciless the picture might be, there would be something in it that suggested that it was dark against some white and blazing background, a background of the astonishment of the angels and the dreadful wonder of God.

The Speaker, July 9th, 1904

*　　*　　*

POETRY AND BELIEFS

You never work so well for art's sake as when you are working for the sake of something else. The greatest of the decadent art-philosophers, in that admirable essay 'The Decay of Lying', described how art could take its disciple through the fires of Dante's perdition and the lilies of Dante's beatitude. But he forgot one point. He forgot that Dante wrote that prodigious thing, not, of course, believing that its story was literally true, but believing that its philosophy was absolutely true and that all counter-philosophies were the lies of devils. Out of the furnace of that certainty came those tremendous things. And, to this day, all our clever irreligious poetry is only the echo of them. Blasphemy itself could not survive religion; if anyone doubts that, let him try to blaspheme Odin. The school which held that literature could be great, independent of convictions, has been free and running about for some thirty years in England and forty in France. Heaven knows its poets have not been hampered by convictions. Has it produced any grander paganisms than that of the man in the tomb of fire? Has it produced any loftier defiance of Omnipotence than that which Milton the Puritan imagined and wrote down? Where are the fruits of its freedom? They are little indeed beside the fruit of that immemorial and sublime bondage.

Daily News, June 25th, 1904

*　　*　　*

TWO GREAT TORIES

Two very great men have only recently passed from us, to all appearances very different – the one a butterfly with a sting, the other a buffalo with a touch of attractive weakness. But Henley and Whistler were, I believe, up to the last friends; and it is good that they should have been friends, for of all men on earth the most pathetic are those who, like them, have a noble talent for finding friends and a noble talent for losing them. Moreover, they stood together on yet greater things. They were both representatives of that great intellectual and artistic reaction which followed the exhaustion of the Liberalism of the French Revolution; they were both what an able writer some days ago called 'strong Illiberals'. They were both Tories; that is, pessimists. Nothing strikes one so much about the attitude of both as the fact that a superb melancholy made it necessary for both to take refuge in something, in something outside current life. Henley took refuge among criminals and Whistler (less happy) among artists; but they were both brave and sad men. Henley as a poet was great only when he uttered the very rhapsody of stoicism. Whistler's whole life was a nocturne; it was like one of his own pictures in which the darkness is lit only with one red or lemon gleam, the Chinese lanterns of art.

Whistler and Henley, amid all their differences, had this essential point in common – that they were both provocative, that they both took a pleasure in putting their views in an extreme form. This is commonly regarded in our country as a mark of frivolity, but it is in truth a mark of faith to joke about one's convictions, to exaggerate them as a proof of their solidity and security; for nobody exaggerates unless he is feeling satisfied and safe. A man dances on a rock, not on a tightrope. The English, however, along with their admirable virtues, have one very impracticable delusion. They tend to think that an extreme course must be unreasonable and that a middle course must be reasonable. This, of course, depends entirely on the nature of the proposal or proposition involved. There are some proposals and propositions in which a middle course is a great deal more insane than either extreme;

but even in these we tend as a nation to adopt the moonstruck compromise. ... But there have been from time to time men among us who have felt that this worship of compromise as compromise was not sensible in the least. They have felt that a position was not necessarily unreasonable because it was consistent and clear. They have felt that a position was not necessarily reasonable merely because it was neither fish, flesh nor herring. They held that if a sane man had views at all, it was part of his sanity to see the views fully and see far into them. In short, they regarded the thing called 'moderation' as one of the cloudiest manias of the asylum. Of these men were Henley and Whistler.

Their main thesis was, of course, that of making art immoral or occasionally (in the case of the more exuberant Henley) anti-moral. As a revolt against a certain form of moral art, common in the Royal Academy, of course they were right enough. A picture of a kindly vicar listening to the violin-playing of a worthy-looking country boy is doubtless evil, but not merely because it is inartistic. It is also evil because it is immoral, because it is full of diabolical snobbishness and cowardice and vulgarity and meanness of spirit. They showed that art was immoral, but only where it happened that morality was immoral.

In truth, the real relation between art and morals is very perfectly exemplified in the case of Whistler and Henley themselves. The real relation between art and morals is merely this, that as both exist in an intelligible world, they exhibit something of the same general laws and phenomena. This is quite a different thing from the defence of the 'anecdotal' picture, which Whistler rightly ridiculed; to say that a picture is a good picture because it exhibits a man giving sixpence to a beggar is quite as absurd as to say that giving the sixpence is wicked if it is done in a red waist-coat with a purple tie. But it may easily happen that the violation of the Divine Law of charity may exhibit parallel symptoms on its own plane, to the violation of God's darker or more mystic canon against red waistcoats.

Let me give an instance. Everyone who has ever amused himself with black and white sketching knows that it is the instinct of the artist to draw much more lightly and softly with a BB pencil than with an HB. But perhaps everyone has not observed the abyss of ethical significance in this fact, the vast effect of it on multitudinous commandments and by-laws, its effect on the Position of Women, on Christian Social Theory, on the late war in South Africa, on the conception of a gentleman and on the politics of Mr Henley. Many a careless young fellow, it may be, has retouched a sketch with a BB without thinking of all this or at least without thinking of it intensely and with tears. A man draws delicately with a strong pencil because the sense of power makes him easy and tactful and gives a pleasure to the thought of gaining great things at a touch. In other words, the idea that the strong are gentle, the idea which in morals is the basis of chivalry and charity, is not a mere sentimental patchwork; it is an actual organic principle of existence, discoverable in dead materials, traceable in a lead pencil and a scrap of paper. The merciful man is not only merciful to his beast, but merciful to his sketching-block, and in both cases because he feels his power. And this truth applies with almost startling accuracy to the two very men we were considering. For this element of a powerful mildness was the one thing lacking in Henley's ethics. And it was the one thing splendidly present in Whistler's art. The great painter's line was never so faint and filmy as when he worked in charcoal or black chalk or such rich and dark substances, capable, if necessary, of painting the hollows of Hell. His touch on the paper was a kind of terrible caress. He seemed at times to have brushed it only with a feather, but the feather was in the wing of an archangel who could have laid the world waste with the whirlwind of his wings. Through the whole runs the great law of force and gentleness which is the same in ethics. Whistler the painter gives what the healthy moralist gives – hints.

Impressionism is but Christianity [applied] to a canvas. And this Christianity was, as I say, the one thing absent in Henley. He had force, but never reserve force; energy but not ease. He wrote with an iron pen, but he never seemed sure that there was enough ink in it. Sometimes it ended, as such exasperating inkless pens end, with a savage scratch. And so the two great men went on saying triumphantly to each other and to the world that art was immoral, that ethics had no place in it, that the true picture was only an arrangement or a symphony. And all the time the very arrangements and symphonies of Whistler were sharp moral criticisms of Henley. Every sketch and scrawl was a personal parable and the great critic might have found in a few grey strokes on white paper the secret of his own unhappy life.

The truth is surely that both schools, the school of the violent ethics of Henley and the school of the touch-and-go art of Whistler, were divided, vastly to their own detriment, by the chaos of the Tory revival. We live in the Tory revival. That is to say, we live in a world in which artists care for nothing but art, and ethicalists for nothing but ethics. The worst of all conceivable curses has fallen upon art, it has become solely artistic; the saddest of all damnations has fallen upon morality, it has become purely moral. There was a time when art and morals together were part of a great general view of life called philosophy or religion. The last appearance of that universal theory was the French Revolution, which defined the rights of man; the last appearance before that was the Christian morality which defined his obligations. But the supreme value of all religion has been this, and it is a value which a man can quite easily feel, even if he cannot admit any religious assumptions. The historic advantage of religion was that it made every part of a man's life, art and ethics and the rest, dependent upon a general view of life itself.

We awake at our birth staring at a very funny place. After serious examination of it we receive two fairly definite impressions; the first, delight and the second, fear. The first leads us to dance and kick about in the sunlight; the second leads us not to do it too much for fear we should get sunstroke. The first leads us, that is to say, to institute festivals and so create art. The second leads us to institute rules and so create morality. One tells us that the praise of the Lord is the beginning of art; the other, that the fear of the Lord is the beginning of wisdom. And in the days of religion, in the days of the Catholic democracy or the Puritan democracy, these two things, however exaggerated in one direction or another, were still parts of a whole. The old rules of moral observance might run to fanaticism or a fantastic scrupulosity; but still they were the laws of God – that is, a part of the All; the old forms and festivals might run to the wildest pageantry and excess, but still they were the praise of God – that is, a part of the All. But in that great breakdown of belief which is the beginning of the new Toryism, they have, for a sign, been totally separated. Law has become cruel in Henley and art supercilious in Whistler – both because they have been separated from the rest of life. Men have become idolatrous towards these things and treated art and morality respectively as gods. For assuredly they are children of God and when God has been eliminated, they may be called, for want of anything better, his heirs. As they look to us today with their melancholy eyes, they may be heirs; they are certainly orphans.

Daily News, August 1st, 1903

* * *

THE FALLACY OF FREEDOM

Anarchism, appeals to absolute liberty, renunciation of limitations as such – all this is incurably futile and childish, because it will not face a fundamental logical fact. This fact is that there is no such thing as a condition of complete emancipation, unless we can speak of a condition of nonentity. What we call emancipation is always and of necessity simply the free choice of the soul between one set of limitations and another. If I have a piece of chalk in my hand, I can make either a circle or a square; that is the sacred thing called liberty. But I cannot make a thing that is both a circle and a square. I cannot make an unlimited square. I cannot draw an emancipated circle. If I wish to make anything at all, I must abide by the limitations and principles of the thing I make. . . . And any man who makes anything whatever, if it be with a piece of chalk, is doing exactly what a man does when he marries or enlists in an army. He is courageously selling himself into a splendid slavery. And, of course, in moral matters it is the same; there is no lawlessness, there is only a free choice between limitations.

Daily News, December 21st, 1905

* * *

LIBERTY

One of the truisms which I was taught from infancy and have only learned in extreme old age is this; that the life of a commonwealth is its liberty. This very word liberty is old-fashioned. You have hardly heard it seriously mentioned as an ideal since the days of Byron and Miss Jane Porter. Now the reason why people in that time talked about liberty was quite simple; it was that they had some. They had tasted, they had even drunk, the dreadful wine. . . .

I am more and more convinced that we have to ask again the old question, 'Is this a free country?' It is still a very rich country; it will always, I think, be a great country; it is everywhere a humorous and in some patches a happy country; and anyhow, it is my country and that is enough for me. But it is not a free country. For some time past it has been losing, first slowly but now rapidly, the last vestiges of that particular thing called freedom.

Loyalty is the heart of the commonwealth; but liberty is its lungs. You find out the necessity of liberty as you find out the necessity of air – by not having enough of it and gasping.

Daily News, March 18th, 1911

*　　　*　　　*

THE SERVILE STATE

When you break the big laws, you do not get liberty; you do not even get anarchy. You get the small laws.

Daily News, July 29th, 1905

*　　　*　　　*

THE SIN OF PROHIBITION

Today a criticism of Prohibition cannot be an attack; it can only be an autopsy. . . . Prohibition has fallen down dead of its own crawling corruption; of the foul humours that infected its own body; and not by any adequate attack from without. It was, if ever there was one, a thing that failed because it had been tried; that found its doom because it had its chance; that was a practical failure because it was a practical fact; that was ruined, not by being frustrated but by being fulfilled; and came to its unnatural end because it had run its natural course. Prohibition died because it was deserted by Prohibitionists; even more than because it was always derided by sensible men and by men with a sense of history and civilization. It is true that there are still various legal entanglements, twisted and re-twisted by the unthinkable fanatics at the feverish moment of their power; but hardly anybody pretends that Prohibition is morally tenable or tolerable today, and indeed it is only a question of whether it is a repealed law or a dead letter. And as the autopsy may well be more elaborate and complete than the attack, I should like to point out especially that the poison that is present in the remains, the poison of which the victim undoubtedly died, is in fact a poison of a certain spiritual sort which is the worst enemy of life.

That poison is sin. And Prohibition perished because the spirit within it is sinful and has the quality of all the sins that destroy the soul. We pay the Prohibitionists far too high a compliment when we call them over-righteous or self-righteous or even Pharisaical. The evil was not really in any exaggeration of ethical seriousness; in the sense, for instance, in which the old Puritan might really be rather unbalanced in his horror at harlotry and the brazen profession of prostitution; or a sensitive person might go a little mad from the mere shock of encountering some madness of moral perversion. The evil of the thing lay much deeper, because it was not a narrowing of the moral sense; it was a violent dislocation and uprooting of the moral sense. The common conscience of sane people is a thing which I and others continue to call the voice of God; but anyhow it is the voice of Man. It is the healthy response of the universal human mind to certain ideas and it does not really differ very widely in its deliberate and conscious decisions; though of course it is modified by particular perils, particular duties of the moment, and the rest. Now if you take a normal person, a nice child, a reasonably trained man, a human being not falling short of the fulness of human nature, you will find that such a person knows that certain decisions are unjust, certain actions cruel, certain risks ordinary, certain matters a man's own business, and so on. Only by perverting his conscience, only by making his mind crooked, can you induce him to believe that drinking beer is something like assassination or betrayal. And by the time that you have succeeded, you have ruined his moral sense. It is no longer a spontaneous spiritual thing; it is no longer a natural thing that can smell evil; it is only capable of repeating a dead, distorted lesson like something imposed by a mesmerist. That mesmerist is not a moralist. He is, in the most emphatic sense, an immoralist. He corrupts the conscience of the young.

Far too little attention has been paid to this point of very practical psychology. You wreck the tribunal of truth when you bribe or bully it into pronouncing the innocent guilty, just as you do when you similarly induce it to pronounce the guilty innocent. As it is with an innocent man, so it is with an innocent practice. You have to destroy all innocence to make anyone detest an innocent practice. By the time that you have persuaded a nice and normal child that it is wicked to fetch his poor old father a glass of ale, you have so bewildered the mind that it may end by saying it is not wicked to put prussic acid in the ale. The logical, mathematical, intellectually inevitable effect of doing this is a general loosening of all morality. It is also the actual effect; and there is the actual state of modern America to prove it. Begin with a heresy in morals, whether it be a negative or a permission, and it will end in the worst and wildest licence that could follow on the loosest permission. And if anyone doubts this psychological fact, which is also a theological truth, then let him explain the howling nightmare and hell of nonsense and anarchy that has actually followed in the track of the Prohibition Law.

True Temperance Quarterly, May, 1933

* * *

AUTOMATIC EVIL

A sophistry may affect the mind, but an obscenity must affect the mind; it is a violence. It may do one of two things equally direct and instinctive; it may shock purity or it may inflame impurity. But in both cases the process is brutal and irrational. A picture or a sentence which shocks sensibility or sharpens sensuality does not offer itself for discussion. It is no more open to argument than a squeaking slate pencil is open to argument, or the choking smell of ether is open to argument. The human victim is drugged – or he is sick.

Therefore (without carrying the parallel, of course, to any lengths of literalism), I think we may speak of indecorum as an assault. In the matter of violations of traditional public decency (however plausibly defended) I am entirely with the Puritans. The ordinary argument that sex can be treated calmly and freely like anything else is the most loathsome cant in this canting epoch. The parallels from other crimes are insolently fallacious. A man reading about a burglary is not any more likely to commit a burglary. A man who has seen a pocket picked is not in the least likely to become a pickpocket. But there is one evil which, by its hold on the imagination (the creative and reproductive part of man), can reproduce itself even by report. We have a right to protect ourselves and especially our top-heavy and groping children against startling and uncivilized appeals to this instinct. Heretics have a legal claim to persuade human souls to err and sin like human souls; they have no business to make them jump like monkeys on a stick. I have no more right to give an unwilling citizen a sexual shock than to give him an electric shock. I have no more right to come behind him and inflame his passions than to come behind him and inflame his coat tails. . . .

The appeal to animal appetite may succeed by its very familiarity. Indecency is not wild and lawless. The danger of indecency is exactly that it is tame, dull, direct, inevitable; a mere law in the members. It is automatic evil. Pride makes a man a devil; but lust makes him a machine.

Daily News, February 19th, 1910

*   *   *

THE TYRANNICAL SCEPTIC

It is a total error to suppose that the possession of convictions – of hard, strong, unquenchable convictions – makes a man bigoted. It is quite the other way. The most bigoted people in the world are the people who have not got any convictions at all. It may seem an extreme or fanciful statement, but it is really true that there are no subjects in the world on which men are so noisy, so aggressive, so violent and angry even unto slaying, as the subjects about which they do not care. ... Men have said that the ground of bigotry is ignorance, but more is true than that: the ground of bigotry is indifference. There is one figure who has dominated history and been the oppressor of all religions, good and bad; all philosophies, true and false. He is the tyrannical sceptic – and his name is Pilate.

Black and White, March 7th, 1903

*　　*　　*

THE SHAPE OF THINGS TO COME

The earnest Freethinkers need not worry themselves so much about the persecutions of the past. Before the Liberal idea is dead or triumphant, we shall see wars and persecutions the like of which the world has never seen. They need not reserve their tears for the victims of Bonner or Claverhouse. They may weep for themselves and for their children.

Daily News, February 18th, 1905

*　　*　　*

SKY SIGNS

The next great heresy is going to be simply an attack on morality; and especially on sexual morality. And it is coming, *not* from a few Socialists surviving from the Fabian Society, but from the living exultant energy of the rich resolved to enjoy themselves at last, with neither Popery nor Puritanism nor Socialism to hold them back. ... The roots of the new heresy, God knows, are as deep as nature itself, whose flower is the lust of the flesh and the lust of the eye and the pride of life. I say that the man who cannot see this cannot see the signs of the times; cannot see even the sky-signs in the street that are the new sort of signs in heaven. The madness of tomorrow is *not* in Moscow but much more in

Manhattan – but most of what was in Broadway is already in Piccadilly.

G. K.'s Weekly, June 19th, 1926

* * *

THE MONSTROSITY

When a dead body is rotting, it does not diminish; it swells. Ignorance of this elementary truth is at the back of nearly all our political blindness. When we speak of a decaying people or a dying institution, we always have somehow the notion of their dwindling; of sparser and sparser tribes gathering on their mountains, of meaner and meaner buildings arising in their skies. But it is not so that social bodies really rot. They rot like physical bodies, being horribly distended from within by revolting gases demanding egress. Institutions, like corpses, grow larger and larger as they grow more and more shapeless. A dying monarchy is always one that has too much power, not too little; a dying religion always interferes more than it ought, not less. Our own country is really in this state of swollen decay, and the test of it is this: that every function of the State has grown more formless and more vast. Every power, public and private, has been stretched long past all sane definition and we live under a government of entangled exaggerations. It is a government that has all the practical effects of anarchy. Indeed, it is something worse than chaos; a warring polytheism. It is a conflict of incalculable autocracies, under any of which at the moment we may fall.

Daily News, March 11th, 1911

* * *

POLITICS AND DISCONTENT

Europe at present exhibits a concentration upon politics which is partly the unfortunate result of our loss of religion, partly the just and needful result of our social inequality and iniquity. These causes, however, will not remain in operation for ever. Religion is returning from her exile; it is more likely that the future will be crazily and corruptly superstitious than that it will be merely rationalist. . . . On the other hand, our attempts to right the extreme ill-balance of wealth must soon have some issue; something will be done to lessen the perpetual torture of incompetent compassion; some scheme will be substituted for our malevolent anarchy, if it be only one of benevolent servitude. And as these two special unrests about the universe and the State settle down into more silent and enduring systems, there will emerge more and more those primary and archaic truths which the dust of these two conflicts has veiled. The secondary questions relatively solved, we shall find ourselves all the more in the presence of the primary questions of man.

For at present we all tend to one mistake; we tend to make politics too important. We tend to forget how huge a part of a man's life is the same under a Sultan and a Senate, under Nero or St Louis. Daybreak is a never-ending glory, getting out of bed is a never-ending nuisance; food and friends will be welcomed: work and strangers must be accepted and endured: birds will go bedwards and children won't, to the end of the last evening. And the worst danger is that in our modern revolt against intolerable accidents we may have unsettled those things that alone make daily life tolerable. . . . There is danger that the social reformer may silently and occultly develop some of the madness of the millionaire whom he denounces. He may find that he has learnt how to build playgrounds, but forgotten how to play. He may agitate for peace and quiet, but only propagate his own mental agitation. In his long fight to get a slave a half-holiday he may angrily deny those ancient and natural things, the zest of being, the divinity of man, the sacredness of simple things, the health and humour of the earth, which alone make a half-holiday even half a holiday or a slave even half a man.

There is danger in that modern phrase 'divine discontent'. There is truth in it also, of course; but it is only truth of a special and secondary kind. Much of the quarrel between Christianity and the world has been due to this fact; that there are generally two truths, as it were, at any given moment, the ingenious, paradoxical truth suitable to some moment of revolt or reaction, and the ancient underlying truism which is nevertheless true all the time. It is sometimes worth while to point out that black is not so black as it is painted; but black is still black, and not white. So with the merits of content and discontent. It is true that in certain acute and painful crises of oppression or disgrace, discontent is a duty, and shame should call us like a trumpet. But it is not true that man should look at life with an eye of discontent, however high-minded. It is not true that in his primary, naked relation to the world, in his relation to sex, to pain, to comradeship, to the grave or to the weather, man ought to make discontent his ideal; it is black lunacy. Half his poor little hopes of happiness hang on his thinking a small house pretty, a plain wife charming, a lame foot not unbearable, and bad cards not so bad. The voice of the special rebels and prophets, recommending discontent, should, as I have said, sound now and then suddenly, like a trumpet. But the voices of the saints and sages, recommending contentment, should sound unceasingly, like the sea.

T. P.'s Weekly, Christmas Number, 1910

*   *   *

AGAINST DIVINE DISCONTENT

I remember hearing a good deal about divine discontent from my early youth; indeed, rather specially in my early youth. For I was born towards the end of the Victorian age, which many writers, strangely enough, imagine to have been a time of conservative placidity and of people content with their stations in life. As a fact, it was exactly the opposite. It was the period during which two modern ideas came into the world and fought; a true idea that we must raise the economic as well as the political status of the poor; and a fake idea that every man must raise his own economic status, even if he kills everybody else and ultimately himself as well. To both of these different things the more earnest Victorians gave the name of 'divine discontent'. But the mistake of the earnest Victorians was that they tried to make a new morality without having studied any really good philosophy. The thing became rhetoric and sentiment, a thing of words; and they got even the words mixed, as in this case.

For the truth is that the one thoroughly bad sort of discontent is divine discontent. We can all sympathize with human discontent. For human discontent means discontent with inhuman conditions. But divine discontent must really mean discontent with divine conditions. And curiously enough, that is exactly what it did mean in the older and wiser theologies and philosophies, where it was rightly branded as the source of all our woe. I am astonished that this simple truth has not been more simply seen. Thus, Mr Bernard Shaw once wrote a little book on the Bible; full of rather crude criticisms, I think, about the Fall and the Flood and the fear of the devil and all the rest. He judges them, of course, in the light of his familiar evolutionary fancy, that the Creator progresses as well as the Creation; indeed, it looks as if the Creation really creates the Creator. I have noted that the moderns lack philosophy. But I do dislike seeing a very clever man so clumsily missing the point; and in the matter of the Bible, the Fall and the Devil and so on, he does entirely miss the point. He tries to apply to such things the general sentiment of revolt which he feels as a Socialist and which any man may quite reasonably feel as a social reformer. But revolt or righteous indignation of *that* sort is always a discontent with bad conditions. The whole point of the spiritual revolt, dealt with in the Bible, is that it is always a revolt against good conditions.

I am not now bothering about Mr Shaw's belief in the Bible. But I repeat that there is such a thing as seeing the point; and this is the point of the old moralities about the rebel angels or the rebellion of Adam. The point of the story of Satan is not that he revolted against being in hell, but that he revolted against being in heaven. The point about Adam is not that he was discontented with the conditions of the earth, but that he was discontented with the conditions of the earthly paradise. That is a totally different idea (and I will add a much deeper idea) than the obvious reasonableness of revolt against gross tyranny. And until it is understood once more, people will go on being discontented even with contentment. The rich will be even more discontented than the poor.

They will explain that theirs is a divine discontent; and divine discontent is the very devil. You will observe that I use the term in a serious theological sense.

New York American, December 15th, 1932

*　　　*　　　*

RELIGION AND REVOLUTION

It has always seemed to me that the problem of religion arises most vividly *after* the problem of politics or economics has been solved. When we have satisfied men about the problem of their living, we shall then be instantly challenged to satisfy them about the problem of their life. Indeed, their depression will not be finally dealt with till we also satisfy them about the problem of their death. Getting rid of the fear of starvation is not getting rid of the fear of death. And how far men feel themselves under the shadow of death, how near death seems to them in the span of their brief life, depends on all sorts of other matters connected with mood or creed or individual condition; but cannot possibly depend on the mere fact of their economic safety. Monks have a small and secure economic support, and feel one way about death; maniacs in asylums have a small and secure economic support, and feel quite another way about it. But those who fear death most and feel most the mutability of things and find their pleasures most poisoned by pessimism are often the most wealthy and luxurious people in the world. They quite frequently fear death, but they not infrequently hate life; and jump off liners or blow out their brains with revolvers. All this realm of reality is not concerned with prosperity, but with happiness. And when an economic revolution, whether reasonable or unreasonable, has given them prosperity, we have still to consider how to give them happiness. . . .

I have always done my best to claim for men this purely economic justice, though I would rather they had it with liberty in the Distributist way than with slavery in the Bolshevist way. But I never thought that filling their stomachs would stop all the movements of their minds. And their minds will still have to deal with two very terrible enemies of man, the one classed as a mere mood and the other as a cosmic conclusion; their names are Boredom and Despair.

New York American, April 1st, 1933

* * *

THE EVIL DAY

I think the time has come when I should say something in favour of Imperialism and Socialism, and it also happens by a delightful coincidence that I have actually thought of something favourable to say.

Anyone who wishes to do justice either to Imperialism or to Socialism should sharply remember the epoch in which they arose, I mean, of course, arose in this country, and recently. They are both as old as human error. Sparta was Socialistic and Babylon was Imperialist ... Now the great thing to be said for these two great exaggerations or heresies (and every heresy is a truth taught out of proportion) is that they were both rebellions against the age in which I was born. The society against which they raised their voices was a very intellectual and artistic society. I have felt its atmosphere and I truly think that if they had been silent, the very stones would have cried out.

This dark period began vaguely about 1870; that end of the great Liberal epoch, the year when Paris fell and when Dickens died. It spreads equally vaguely up to the retirement of Gladstone and the abandonment of Home Rule, the last Liberal crusade that was unmistakably Liberal and unmistakably dangerous. All that period was filled with emptiness. Oscar Wilde was justly its greatest man; because he alone could really do levity on a large scale. Its products include many men whom I count as my best friends – myself among others. But I can hardly think of one of them who would not have been both better and happier if he had been born in any other period from the Stone Age to the Reign of Terror. For almost all other ages have set one enthusiasm against another; but of this brief and black age only can it be said that it sneered at enthusiasm simply for being enthusiastic. All men had dreaded the lightning because it was destruction; but these disdained the lightning because it was the light.

It is idle presumably to speculate as to the causes of this queer interregnum and vacuum. The truth, I fancy, is this: that religion and politics (man's chief concerns, almost his only concerns) alternate in history, but are seldom absent simultaneously. A rude society may be rich in saints; or a time of frigid infidelity, such as the eighteenth century, may be heroic in politics. But at the particular point I speak of, both these waves were spent. ... The impression was that heavy hands had shut the doors of man's two great outlets – liberty and faith; the one was blocked by Bismarck with his blood and iron, and the other by Darwin with his blood and bones. The appearance of 1870 was that political materialism had broken political idealism for ever. And the appearance of 'The Descent of Man' was that it was really a descent of man – that man had been kicked off his pedestal on to the floor.

Whether for this cause or some other, the years of which I speak were years of yawning; they were like the hours of an afternoon 'At Home' in a rich house on a rainy day when nobody comes to call. Their poems and pictures showed a real genius in tracing the leaden tints and echoing the tuneless tones of an afternoon like that. One hardly heard anything but pessimism – except Art, which is worse. Now whenever I wish to feel tender towards Imperialists or Socialists, I always remember that at least their Union Jacks and their red ties interrupted the twilight of that infernal afternoon. ... Rudyard Kipling did show that romance could be found in coarse and laborious affairs. And the Socialists have at least done one excellent thing; they have brought back creeds into politics. ... For a creed is the sword of the spirit; the only tool with which the mind can fight.

That empty time is now so utterly forgotten that many even who lived in it will hardly know of what I speak. Of its weary wits and philosophic dandies hardly one remains. Some are dead; some have gone into exile; some have gone to pieces. Two I know who were of real genius, a genius which survived that season of ashes and went on burning into our own time. ... One of them was a small vivid man, one of the black Scotch, with dark burning eyes and a high colour. He had been the most piercing lyrist of the old minor poets, but of late he had taken up newer notions, going in with Mr Shaw for enormous images of the Superman or the last giants of evolution. His talk was all of expanding life and unceasing activity. The other was a quieter and much cleverer man; one of the most perfectly clever men ever born. He was tall, slow, saturnine, an omnivorous observer, a very fastidious judge. His work was almost wholly in a world of cool and almost heartless comedy. He had a slight smile always on his face. He also had dropped the mere pessimism of the dark age and was doing hopeful and constructive work in the creation of a new and more solid English drama.

These are the only two men who have come triumphant out of that strange old atmosphere. Each of them during the last few months has died by his own hand.

Daily News, June 26th, 1909

[The two men were John Davidson, the poet, and St John Hankin, the dramatist.]

*   *   *

WHAT WAS RATIONALISM?

What Rationalism really was and (in some corners) still is, is substantially this: It was a premature synthesis. It was not the opening of the house of reason, but the impatient closing of it. It did not open the human head like a new hotel. It shut the human head like a packed bag. I call it the Victorian Compromise because it put in the bag as many of the old relics and reverences as it could. I call it the Victorian Rationalism because it was guided in its selection by a very clear but very crude theory. In other words, it planned out the packing scientifically, but it never asked whether the bag was big enough. And the result on which I want specially to insist was this; that this false finality of the reason has left behind it a prolonged and increasing torture to the instincts. That is what I mean when I say that Dickens rebelled against it ignorantly and by the light of nature. That is why the war against it was a war of poets, sometimes as irrational as a war of criminals. Ever since Rationalism became the rule, the mysterious thing called human nature has scratched like a cat in a cupboard. ... The Rationalist was pursued by enemies, blind but strong; the most terrible enemies a man has – the things he has forgotten.

New Witness, March 20th, 1913

*   *   *

FROM DICKENS TO GISSING

The tribute paid by George Gissing to Charles Dickens was one of that great tribune and poet of the people, because it was a of that great tribune and poet of the people, because it was a message from the antipodes. It was a compliment to Dickens, not from a Dickensian, but rather from one who might well be expected to be an Anti-Dickensian. Gissing was a realist whose realism is not even enlivened by a controversy about coarseness. The suburban world he describes seems a hundred times more common by not being vulgar. He is also one of those in whom the depression at the end of the nineteenth century had not even the energy to turn into a dance of death, but only into a life too dull for dancing. His carnation turned grey and not green. But he was a man of clear and acute mind, of solid and splendid intellectual honesty; and in spite of his realism, he was in touch with reality. He did see things as they are and therefore saw Dickens as he is; a great wind and a flame and a spirit creating like a god. . . .

The change from Dickens to Gissing is among other things an economic or at least a sociological change. It marks the difference between the men who built the industrial town and the men who were born in it. Or to put it another way, it is the contrast between the jovial swagger with which the young man from the country came to London and the gloom that settled upon him when he really discovered that he could never get back to the country. It is generally supposed, for instance, that the clerks and comic servants in Dickens are mere flights of his own poetic fancy. But it is not altogether so. In this and other things there is a great deal of exaggeration about his exaggeration. There was a type to be exaggerated, and nowadays it is not exaggerated because it is not there. It was the sort of Cockney who was not only exuberant but solemnly and rhetorically exuberant; relishing romantic poetry and rolling words. My father told me of an aged clerk in an ancient eating-house who regularly every day said to the waiter in a deep booming voice, 'Tell Mrs Bayfield that the steak was excellent, the potatoes done to a turn, in short, a dinner fit for an epicure'. That is the voice of Micawber and Swiveller and many characters of Dickens; even of Fred Bayham and many characters of Thackeray. And who will ever forget the schoolmaster who said to every lady he danced with, 'Had I a heart for falsehood framed, I ne'er could injure you'? It is the great gusto; it is life enjoyed like the steak of Mrs Bayfield; existence as something much too joyful to be taken frivolously; enjoyment as something to be prolonged with a prodigious gravity; in short, a dinner fit for an epicure. After a hundred modern criticisms there remains in the poetry of Byron and Tom Moore, which these men quoted, a richness that has never been recovered or imitated. Many moderns have learnt from Yeats that our souls are love and a continual farewell; but not many can say farewell to Miss Wackles with the great and virile gesture: 'My boat is on the shore and my barque is on the sea.' Men naturally made game of the Byronic youth; but remember that he enjoyed woe more than the moderns enjoy enjoyment.

Now by the time of Gissing we are beginning to get into the world of Wells. The small stumpy heroes of Wells are still courageous, but the courage is almost the courage of despair. It seems as if they were stumpy through being stunted by a bludgeoning from above. And indeed they have felt the full weight of the club of the giant called Capitalism. They can still joke; but when they joke, they jeer and even sneer. I know there is plenty to sneer at; and that the little man's bitter tongue is the only sword we have left him. But certainly he does sneer, not to say snarl. And Sam Weller never snarled; he never even sneered. It was all unlike his great and gracious ways; it was quite beneath his dignity. But then Sam Weller felt free; he had run loose and been a waggoner's boy and many things, and travelled from inn to inn and job to job; he had never felt the weight of the modern terror, pinning a man to one place which it is ruin to lose. For in that old England there was indeed no equality, but there was liberty; an instinct in poor and rich alike for letting people wander and take their chance. Hence the string of episodes in the *Pickwick Papers* and the general feeling that London cannot contain or control the characters. I think there is something of it even in the mere change in illiterate speech that has often been noted as separating us from Sam Weller. In modern Cockney, I am sorry to say there is not only something of a snarl; there is something very like a whine. It has its masterpieces of irony; it is a good speech for satirists, but it is not quite a speech for free men. Now the old Weller dialect is said by some to have been the Kentish dialect, and certainly it is as rich and deep as the gardens of Kent. In that interchange of V's and W's there is something of swagger, something of waggishness, but something also of leisure and ease. . . .

But in any case the Weller dialect, whether or not it was a county dialect, was in spirit a country speech. It was a speech that had grown luxuriant and even long-winded in long hours of talk in the taverns of the age of toleration. Its very jokes were in a manner ceremonial. The jokes of the later generation consist entirely of what is appropriately called chipping; and they are very small chips of that old block, of that original Yule-log of the Pickwick period. And, as I say, I think there is something of it even in the sound and style of the slang. Those waggish W's suggest only a slight laxity and, according to the lateness of the hour, perhaps indistinctness in the edges of the spoken word. They have nothing of the snigger or the whine. Sir John Falstaff was a gentleman by birth; but I can almost imagine even Falstaff saying with his thick accent, 'What, because you are wirchuous shall there be no more cakes and ale?' But I cannot imagine Falstaff saying, 'Shall there be no more cikes and ile?'. . . .

I believe the explanation of the change is that which I have given; the fact that by the later date the traveller no longer stopped at London as an inn, but found himself caught in London as in a trap; a network of communications snaring him like a net. Shades of the prison house began to close in more senses than one; but poor Gissing was really more imprisoned in Fleet Street than Pickwick in Fleet Prison. The economic element begins to be exaggerated and literature begins to deal with livelihood rather than life.

But Gissing's book is a monument of the fact that literature can almost always understand literature, and that the world which a man appreciates is wider than the world he describes. For what the realist critics forgot was that the world exactly reproduced by Gissing will vanish much more completely than the world exaggerated by Dickens. Life as described in Pickwick is much more like life as described in *Don Quixote* or in the *Canterbury Tales* or in the *Odyssey* or even in the Bible, than like in a psychological novel of the suburbs; because it refers to fundamentals, travels and inns and simple jokes. It is like life; it is in that sense like eternal life, for it is still alive.

G. K.'s Weekly, October 17th, 1925

*　　*　　*

The Corner

Modern England cannot live any longer on that old compromise of Queen Victoria, loyalty and liberty, Anglicanism and agnosticism, Lord Tennyson and the party system. It was a generous age; it was a liberal and honourable age; we all owe everything to it. There was something about its innocent assumption of all good things at once, its combination of all the inconsistent virtues, that will always remind us of a home. But it is no house for us any longer. We have gone down a road; and we have turned a corner.

Daily News, May 14th, 1910

*　　*　　*

Chaos

Humanity has passed through every sort of storm and shipwreck, but never before was it so doubtful which was the storm and which the shipwreck, and which the ship and which the ship's crew; and what we are rescuing from what.

New York Herald Tribune Magazine, July 5th, 1931

*　　*　　*

THE VENGEANCE OF VICTORIA

Nobody has yet appreciated the post-Victorian Age; our histories do not yet record that it has begun; they could hardly be expected to record that it has ended. The young are still flaunting their superiority to Victorianism which died a quarter of a century ago. They do not realize that Victorianism was itself immensely superior to that much more powerful thing that only died yesterday. The thing I mean might be broadly indicated by many names. Perhaps the most popular way of putting it would be to say that the Victorian Age was followed by the American Age. The Age of Public Opinion, which meant only the things the middle classes thought or believed, was followed by the Age of Publicity, which meant the loud assertion of things that nobody believed. The age in which the middle-class man was supposed to be content to be middle class or even rather stodgily proud of being middle class, was followed by a sort of feverish Utopia of unrest in which every middle-class man was idiot enough to suppose he could become a millionaire. The age of port, in which men drank after dinner, was followed by the age of cocktails, in which women had to get drunk in order to face the prospect of dinner. All that has happened since the death of Victoria. It has begun since the death of Victoria. It has died since the death of Victoria. For there will not even be any money for it much longer. But it has died so recently that nobody has given it any epitaph; nobody has even given it a name.

On all that sort of thing poor old Queen Victoria has already been avenged. It is perfectly self-evident that Victorianism, with all its vices, was vastly superior to the thing which so rapidly sprang up in its place and so rapidly withered in its place. For instance, Victorian morality, passing from Puritanism to Positivism, did not understand much of the mystical sort of humility. But it did understand something of the ordinary manly sort of modesty; the decent restraint known to pagans like the Romans or the Chinese. It was followed by a mere lunatic asylum of lying and bragging that was called advertisement and salesmanship; with the final financial result that nothing can be sold and that all the money for advertisement has been wasted. It was the post-Victorians who went in for mere go-getting; and it has gone no-where and got nothing. We have all heard of a famous occasion when Queen Victoria was not amused. But I fancy that even she might be amused now.

G. K.'s Weekly, October 15th, 1932

*   *   *

PRIVACY

Privacy is like property in this: that while a few people ought to have less of it, most people ought to have more of it.

New Witness, October 7th, 1921

*   *   *

NORTHCLIFFE

It is perfectly apparent that Alfred Harmsworth never had any ideas at all. He must have had intelligence in the business sense; and something much more valuable in business, that sort of natural heat and hurry which can work too fast to think of why it is working. He was not without his good points; perhaps it would be more exact to say that he was not without his good moments, for he had no conceptions clear enough to perpetuate them at the expense of the bad ones. He did pay his proletariat better than many; he did do good-natured as well as ill-tempered things. Also he had everything against him in the intellectual and moral sense. He was born of respectable middle-class people in the small Protestant professional classes in Dublin. He received in succession all the general political suggestions of his time. He was thrilled by Jameson and Joe Chamberlain; he apparently believed up to the very moment of the Great War that there was a place called Ulster. In other words, he had at the best all the healthy and hazy associations and prejudices which all his ten million readers had as much as he had; and he was by nature ignorant of the very idea of an idea. But while Alfred Harmsworth was exactly like Albert Huggins or any other man travelling in the same train or tube, there came upon him to his destruction two things that were not normal to the rest. He became enormously rich which always cuts a man off from reality. And he dealt, not in his native elements like pork or petrol, but in politics and public opinion. He bought a pulpit from which ideas could have been given, when he had no ideas to give. . . .

An excellent example of all these things is to be found in the business about Lord Kitchener. . . . The truth is that Harmsworth never had anything to do with Kitchener at all. He had to do with a sort of legendary bully who was only to be admired for bullying, and then with an equally legendary dug-out to be dismissed because he was not in a hurry to bully. It was a great stunt to declare that a strong man stood ready to save England; a great stunt to declare that England was betrayed. The real story of the shell shortage was something totally different; but that story would never have made a stunt. It is typical of him that as soon as he had left off cheering for the mere name of Kitchener, and then left off booing at the mere name of Kitchener, he began cheering again at the mere name of Lloyd George. No real person ever appeared in his portrait gallery. But dull megalomania of this sort is always vaguely impressed by a stupid swagger in others. Dullness calls unto dullness across the modern world, like deep calling unto deep. . . .

It was perhaps this spirit of illusion, of indirect rather than direct things, that produced in his mind the tragedy of the final divorce from reality. None will deny that such a tragedy should teach us to consider him as a human being; but the sympathy is thwarted by considering him as a hero. It was the fault of his age rather than himself that he lived among shadows, fighting in a shadow pantomime. Publicity consists, not of things, but of their vast shadows thrown upon a wall. And to make them so vast, the light must be held very low down.

G. K.'s Weekly, September 17th, 1927

*   *   *

The Vision of Vulgarity, I

Vulgarity is one of the great new modern inventions, like the telephone or the wireless set. It may be plausibly maintained that the telephone is less of an instrument of torture than the thumbscrew or the rack; and in the same way that other ages had other vices that were worse than this new or modern vice. As we may find fanciful sketches of aeroplanes in the sketch-books of Leonardo da Vinci or speculations very near to modern physics in the philosophers of ancient Greece, so we may find here and there in history a hint or foreshadowing of the great and golden vision of Vulgarity that was later to burst on the world. We may find it in the smell of Punic plutocracy that stank in the nostrils of Greeks and Romans, or in a certain touch of bad taste in an aesthete like Nero. Nevertheless, the thing is so new that the new world has not yet really found a name for it, but has had to borrow a rather misleading name which is really the Latin word for something else. So we have to go on using the Greek name of amber as the only name of electricity, because we have no notion what is the real name or nature of electricity. And so we have to go on using the Latin word *vulgus*, which only means the common people, to describe something that is not particularly common among the common people. Indeed, through long spaces of human history and over wide spaces of the habitable globe, it is very uncommon amongst the common people. Farmers living by long agricultural traditions, peasants in normal villages, even savages in savage tribes, are hardly ever vulgar. Even when they massacre and enslave, even when they offer human sacrifice or eat human flesh, they are hardly ever vulgar. All travellers attest the natural dignity of their carriage and the ceremonial gravity of their customs. Even in the more complex modern cities and civilizations, the poor as such are not particularly vulgar. No; there is a new thing which really needs a new name and still more a new definition. I do not say I can define Vulgarity; but having just been reading a modern book about Love, I feel inclined to throw out a few suggestions.

In so far as I can get near to its essence, it consists largely of two elements, which I should describe as Facility and Familiarity.

The first means that a man does, as the phrase goes, 'gush'; that is, that his self-expression flows without effort, selection or control. It does not come from him like picked or pointed words, passing through an articulate organ; it simply streams from him like perspiration. He need never stop explaining himself, for he understands neither himself nor the limits of explanation. He is the sort of man who understands women; he is the man who can always get on with the boys; he finds it easy to talk, easy to write, easy to speak in public; for his own self-satisfaction carries with it a sort of huge cloud and illusion of applause.

And the second element is Familiarity which, if understood, would be called Profanity. Horace spoke of the 'profane vulgar'; and it is true that this familiarity is the loss of holy fear and a sin against the mystical side of man. In practice it means handling things confidently and contemptuously, without the sense that all things in their way are sacred things. Its most recent mode is the readiness to write torrents of tosh on either side of any serious subject; for you hardly ever get *real* vulgarity on a frivolous subject. The point is that the fool is so subjective that it never occurs to him to be afraid of the subject. For instance, he can be a Pagan fool as well as a Puritan fool in the debate on modern morals; but in the first case there will be torrents of tosh about Love and Passion and the Right to Live, and in the other, exactly similar torrents of tosh about Christian Manhood and Healthy Boyhood and Noble Motherhood and the rest. The trouble is that they are so infernally familiar with these things. Never do you find that note in a real lover writing of the woman he loves, or in a real saint writing of the sin he hates. Both say the right thing because they would rather say nothing at all.

New York American, July 22nd, 1933

*   *   *

THE VISION OF VULGARITY, II

I do not know very much about the movement or institution covered by the title of Toc H. But I know the man who inspired

it, my old schoolfellow Philip Bayard Clayton; and though some
of my other friends have differed from some of its sociology, I am
quite sure that in him and his immediate following the movement
was generous and genuine. And I can testify that on one occasion
of my attending its meetings, the ceremony commemorating those
dead in the war was as decent and reticent and virile a thing
as I ever knew. It was the only satisfactory modern ceremonial
that I ever knew. I liked it all the better because it was not in the
loose modern sense religious. It was made up by soldiers among
themselves, and it might have been made by noble heathens in the
antique world. So far as I remember, it was merely the burning out
of a candle and, when it was extinguished, someone saying those
lines of Laurence Binyon which are worthy to pass into an im-
personal and immortal rite.

> They shall grow not old, as we that are left grow old:
> Age shall not weary them, nor the years condemn.
> At the going down of the sun and in the morning
>   We will remember them.

That was all, and that was a good thing to remember.

Now I open the large Sunday paper of the *Express* group and
the first thing that knocks me in the eye is a huge headline about
the Toc H ceremony as recently conducted. It is an announcement
in gigantic letters 'D.S.O. Sobs at Ceremony' and immediately
underneath in slightly smaller letters, 'Prince of Wales Lights the
Lamp'. The journalist does print the words of Mr Binyon's poem;
but as he prints them in prose, he is presumably unaware that they
are verse. I do not expect him to be aware that they are poetry.
He takes his place with that celebrated journalist who wrote, 'The
right hon. gentleman concluded by saying that kind hearts were
in his opinion better than coronets and simple faith greatly prefer-
able to Norman blood'. Only in the older case there was more
excuse; for I cannot but think the poetry was more prosaic. Tennyson could be Virgilian like Laurence Binyon; but I should hardly
select that passage to prove it.

Now if it be asked what I dislike in the domination of this type
of Trust journalism, I answer that I dislike 'D.S.O. Sobs' and the

man who does not dislike 'D.S.O. Sobs' and the domination of the man who is capable of writing 'D.S.O. Sobs' and the type of society that is supposed to be impressed favourably with 'D.S.O. Sobs' and the whole hideous idea of human pathos which insults you and me with the supposition that 'D.S.O. Sobs' could conceivably move us to anything but mirth or murder. And if the journalist does not understand it, all the more do I protest against the power and influence of the man who does not understand it. And if anybody says he does like it, all the more do I weep and wail over the existence of anybody who does like it. If it was untrue, I denounce it; and if it was true, I denounce it more. My tradition makes no treaty with the man who could first spy on a man's tears then elaborately note his rank, and then clump the two things in colossal letters at the top of the column before he had even told the story; hallooing his remarkable good luck as if he had seen a shark off Margate or the man who broke the bank at Monte Carlo. It is because that is the tone of the Trust and all its literature and view of life that I hope to withstand it till I die. Coarseness about coarse things is not vulgar. It is not in itself immoral; it is in various degrees improper or inexpedient according to conditions and occasion and, above all, motive. But anyhow, to talk grossly about a gross topic is not necessarily to be in the least a vulgarian. But to talk grossly about a sensitive and austere topic, to speak loudly about something that remains in high-strung silence like a harp string, to discover what is deliberately invisible and gape at it, to hear what cannot be spoken and bellow it – this is the shame not to be found among rude and simple men. It is nowhere in the popular tales or traditions; it is not found in the old ballads or the Christmas carols; it is a mixture of weak curiosity and strained attention and a stunted mind and an idiot light-heartedness, which is altogether peculiar to our civilization. . . . We alone have had the honour of producing this fine flower of progress. And this flower will overrun our garden like a weed, when that culture has fully come into its own.

G. K.'s Weekly, January 1st, 1927

*   *   *

THE HUMBLEST ANIMAL

It is in the nature of man to find symbols outside himself of the qualities within himself. Thus, for instance, he has divided his virtues among the beasts of the field. He makes the lion represent bravery; yet men are braver than lions. No lions are ever burnt for their opinions. He makes the fox the type of cunning; yet men are more cunning than foxes. No fox has ever thought of getting on a horse's back to travel faster. He makes the ant a symbol of industry; but he is himself a stronger symbol of industry. He speaks of dog-like fidelity; it would be more emphatic to speak of man-like fidelity. Men are merrier than larks and much more hypocritical than crocodiles. But we men cannot see ourselves as the great things that we are, and perhaps it is our greatness that we cannot. Perhaps this fantastic modesty is the highest of the attributes of man. Perhaps, amid the arrogance of oysters and the self-sufficiency of snails, man is the only humble animal.

Daily News, March 21st, 1906

* * *

PUTTING THE CLOCK BACK

In the present and the quite recent past we see a débris of effects of which we do not know the causes. The fire is choked with its own ashes, the fountain is sealed with its own ice; the original purpose of the thing does not pierce through. The only way to deal with it is to go back and ask what the thing in question – a throne or a theory or a vote – was primarily supposed to be. Nine times out of ten the only way of really building the future is to imagine yourself in some much ruder society in the remote past. You may call this reactionary and barbaric if you choose, just as you can call it reactionary and barbaric to take a bath. Taking a bath certainly involves the removal of many civilized externals and an invitation to the nakedness of savages. But it is the only way to get clean.

Illustrated London News, July 8th, 1911

* * *

The Number You First Thought Of

They that go about the world asking riddles and doing puzzles (those enemies of the human race) used to have one particular game which, after ramifications of arithmetic, ended with 'taking away the number you first thought of'. It is a silly game and, like many other silly games, has been played by great empires and on a large scale. That touch of over-civilization which is always the first touch [*sic*] of a returning barbarism can best be noted whenever we note this game of subtracting the original thought with which everything began. I mean that men will build up institutions and elaborations round the central pillar of some thought. Then, after the passage of centuries, the central pillar falls down, but the rest of the edifice remains. Such an edifice is not always in danger, but it is in decay.

Our forefathers in the morning of the world appear in certain ancient and, as I think, eternal attitudes; in the posture of the performance of certain primal human acts; such as hunting or dancing or feasting or sacrificing to the gods. It is right and natural that these things should grow richer and more complex with time. But it is decadent and dangerous when these things forget their origin and alter their inmost nature; when, after a stretch of centuries, they have turned into something else, sometimes into something opposite.

In order to avoid the fascinating topics of drink and religion, let us take the case of hunting. Sport has silently and subtly reversed its old character. The essence of the change is this; that men began with the comparatively generous idea of killing wild beasts and have ended up with the comparatively paltry idea of preserving them. ... I do not mean to indicate that I think it wrong to preserve or shoot birds; I do not. I merely use this reversal of the heroic in hunting as an instance of the way in which over-elaborate societies end up with their tails in their mouths; in a posture not merely twisted, but inverted.

Of course, there are other instances. There was the primitive man offering sacrifice to the gods. The sacrificer builds an altar and pours wine or blood or something on it and holds up his hands to the sky and talks to somebody he can't see. Then, as time goes on, he turns his remarks into an ordered chant and then, perhaps, into a written book; and he has a roof to cover the people who come to see him sacrifice, and a lectern to read the book from, and a sort of forum or pulpit to stand in and explain what he had been doing, and so on. And then, when civilization has grown for some centuries, there comes an Ethical Society – the advance guard of barbarism. You may know it by this extraordinary fact; that it doesn't take away the additions and excretions round the old human thing; it takes away the old human thing itself. It leaves the reading-desk and the talking-box and the people sitting still on hard seats. But it takes away the altar. It takes away the God. It takes away the number it first thought of.

I might have given many other examples of this turning a thing tail foremost, of this subtraction of the original aim. I have given the case of the hunter who is now chiefly concerned to preserve the very creatures which he set out to destroy. I have given the case of the Ethical Idealist, a really reverent person, who still insists on kneeling even when he has nothing to kneel to. I can only suggest that in this train of thought will really be found a clue in the criticism of the modern world, which is first and last a topsy-turvy world. That is why the few mild and rational people are accused of standing on their heads.

Illustrated London News, February 24th, 1912

*   *   *

The Living Past

If we want in any shape or sense what is commonly called progress, then we must stick to tradition. If you want practical experiments, alterations and improvements, then you must cling convulsively to the past. Read new books if you want an artistic sensation of novelty, a feeling that you are smelling a fresh flower, but not if you want anything done in legislation or social reform; for tradition is the only thing that ever does anything. Read old books if you want new Blue Books.

Man is an animal with his feet foremost and his face turned

back. I defy anyone to mention any plain case of what is ordinarily called progress in human history in which the mind of the progressive people was not specially fixed upon some ideal in the past. Of the Renaissance I need not speak; the very word Renaissance proves the point. But the French Revolution is quite as clear a case; it was founded upon a theory of primitive right and it was perpetually taking for its model the old pagan republics. Rousseau's theory of the social contract was purely an appeal to our human past; recent thinkers doubtless deny that human past, but most of them are sufficiently logical to deny democracy as well. There has not been actually any progress anywhere without some passionate admiration of the past. . . . Man is like Perseus; he cannot look at the Gorgon of the future except in the mirror of the past. All those who have tried to look at a fixed future directly have been turned to stone. The human heart has been petrified in them. The old Calvinists, with their predestination and necessity, were turned to stone. The modern scientific sociologists, with their anthropology and their absurd eugenics, are turned to stone. They make amusing statues.

It is utterly useless to talk about enlarging one's mind with visions of the future. The future does not enlarge one's mind in the least. The future is a blank wall on which I paint my own portrait as large as I like. . . . We are attracted to the future because it is what is called a soft job. In front of us lies an unknown or unreal world which we can mould according to every cowardice or triviality in our own temperaments. But if we look back at our fathers, as they gather in the gate of history, we see it like the gate of Eden described by one of them in verse which we cannot imitate:

'With dreadful faces thronged and fiery arms'.

Daily News, December 7th, 1907

*   *   *

THE UNCHANGING VISION

The principle of progress in which all sane men believe is mainly this: that we are engaged and ought to be engaged in a persistent effort to change the external world into the image of something that is within ourselves; to turn what is, as far as we are concerned, a chaos into what shall be, as far as we are concerned, a cosmos. God did not give us a universe, but rather the materials of a universe. The world is not a picture, it is a palette. Most of us who can remember our childhood at all will agree that the best present that can be given to a child on his birthday is in all probability a paint-box. Many fathers know this; the Father of us all knew it well. He gave man a paint-box. He gave him the crude materials of something; the crude materials of everything. That brown earth beneath you is only raw umber, which you are destined to turn into cooked umber. That blue sea which you think spherical and perfect, is only the element and beginning of something beyond the sea. How gratifying it is to reflect that the word 'ultramarine' literally means 'something beyond the sea'! That green grass is only the material out of which you may make elves and foresters and the figure of Robin Hood. That blood-red sunset which you unwisely call perfect is nothing but a lake of crimson (called for the sake of brevity crimson lake) from which you may fish up the flaming images of purple seraphims and scarlet devils. Heaven gave us this splendid chaos of colours and materials. Heaven gave us a few instinctive rules of practice and caution corresponding to 'do not put the brush in the mouth'. And Heaven gave us a vision.

Now, to make the real world in any way like our vision of it requires an agony of toil, extended over many years and centuries. My own sympathies are all with sudden and decisive change when it can possibly be obtained; but the complete transformation of nature into the vision of a man can only be obtained slowly, if, indeed, it can be obtained at all. Therefore there does come into the realm of ideas the thing called progress. It may be that we shall never reach perfection, but we may continue to approach it. But even if we only approach it, we must believe that it exists, we must believe that there is some comprehensible statement of what it is and where it is. It is important to know where Brighton is, whether

I want to go to Brighton or only towards Brighton. If Brighton has no place or meaning at all, how can I even aim at it? It may be that my human strength will be exhausted before I reach Brighton. It may be that the earth will be burnt up in the sun long before I reach Brighton. It may be that inexorable and awful laws of human limitation keep an armed watch round Brighton and that I can never see the shining gates of that city until I become more than man. But certainly it is just as important to know what Brighton is in order to try to get there, as it is in order to get there after all. And the human race (in the main) has always believed that it knew the broad facts about the site and approachability of Brighton.

When I say Brighton, I use a close metaphor for the New Jerusalem. Men have always believed that, however long or however short might be the time required to reach perfection, perfection had certain clear recognizable lines about it. It would involve justice; it would involve mercy; it would involve truth; it would involve courage. Our attempts to reach this might jump about. But Brighton would not jump about. We should now use this colour, now that colour, of our cosmic paint-box to produce the proper effect. But our vision would not alter. We should always have in our minds the picture that we wanted. Thousands of years ago a great poet put the perfect vision of mercy. 'The lion shall lie down with the lamb.' It will take us a long time to teach him to do it.

But in our own time another and quite different thing has happened. The vision has been attacked, not the picture. The thing we are aiming at is everywhere challenged. Mercy is denied. Justice is denied. The object of all our sacrifices is being talked of as dubious. Brighton is jumping about. It would take many generations (perhaps) of philosophical lion-tamers to induce the lion to lie down with the lamb. But it clearly cannot be done at all if every other generation of lion-tamers thinks that it is not worth doing.

The whole matter, then, can be put in one statement. So long as there is constancy in ideals, there can be progress towards those ideals. The moment there is change in those ideals, the progress, always difficult, becomes impossible. If there is progress in ideals, there cannot be progress in anything else.

Daily News, September 15th, 1906

*   *   *

THE WHITE HOUSE

All conservatism goes upon the assumption that if you leave a thing alone, you leave a thing as it is. But you do not. If you leave a thing to itself, you are leaving it to wild and violent changes. All nature is change; it is only man (apart from religious ideas) whose name is constancy. For instance, if you want a white house, you must not leave it white. If you leave it white in our atmosphere, it will soon be black. If you want a white house, you must continually be painting it white, beginning all over again and re-creating your ideal. In other words, if you want your old white house, you must have a new white house. You must have a revolution. . . .

The foundation of the true doctrine of progress is that all things tend to get worse. Man must perpetually interfere to resist a natural degeneration; if man does not reform a thing, Nature will deform it. He must always be altering the thing even in order to keep it the same. If a man wants to keep his garden the same, he does not leave it to itself, for left to itself it will become quite different. If he wants it to remain the same, he goes about it with a ferocious speed, uprooting things like a walking revolution. For the man who weeds plays the part of a pitiless and positive uprooter. In other words, he plays the part of a Radical. The trimness and tidiness of all our gardens depends upon a persistent Radicalism; and all those ranked flowers and rigid lawns are kept clear and quiet by a principle of perpetual revolution. Similarly, every spring cleaning is a revolution but, like all others, a conservative revolution. Like all other revolutions, it disturbs, maddens, destroys and may even degrade. But its object is to give a man his old clean house, whereas otherwise he would have a new house and a nasty one. The white house must be washed or painted at the first hint of grey.

Now it is specially the misfortune of England for the last few hundred years that we have left our institutions untouched under the impression that we were leaving them unspoilt; whereas, in truth, time and circumstances were steadily spoiling them. We have prided ourselves on being conservative; but in fact we have not even conserved. We would not alter our institutions for the better and so Social Evolution (bless its heart) has altered them for the worse. ... For the whole advantage of evil is in its being so often imperceptible and silent; evil comes at leisure like the disease; good comes in a hurry like the doctor. Conservatives commonly denounce a revolution as premature; it is Irish, but true, to say that a revolution must often come prematurely or come too late.

Daily News, August 24th, 1907

*　　*　　*

THE ICONOCLAST

In the whole range of human occupations is it possible to imagine a poorer thing to be than an iconoclast? It is the lowest of all the unskilled trades.

Daily News, April 26th, 1905

*　　*　　*

THE RETURN OF THE ANGELS

I write these remarks with one great hope, that of arousing controversy. It is really a singular matter that amid all the talk of the great work of physical science and its alleged victory over religious dogmatism, no one has noticed what the greatest of all the triumphs of science really was. It was a discovery far greater than that of evolution. It was the discovery, not of a fact, but of a method, the mother of innumerable facts. That method is, of course, what is known in scientific theory as the method of the hypothesis. It can be most clearly and simply conveyed in common language by saying that it is the principle that the best way to see if a coat fits a man is not to measure both of them, but to try it on. It is the replacing of the very slow, logical method of accumulating, point

by point, an absolute proof by a rapid, experimental and imaginative method which gives us, long before we can get absolute proof,
a very good working belief. I hear, let us say, of a certain theory
about the universe. As a trial, I assume it to be true; then, if I
discover with a start that, once assumed, it explains the boots on
my feet and the nose on my face, that my umbrella has a new and
radiant meaning, that my front door suddenly explains itself, that
truths about my cat and dog and wife and hat and sideboard
crowd upon me all day and every day, I believe that theory and go
on believing it more and more.

On the other hand, if the theory be not true, I may be perfectly
certain that ten minutes after I have experimentally assumed it, I
shall break my shins over some contradiction. We have buttoned
the coat round the world (that rotund and patient old gentleman)
and it has split down the back. It is surely quite obvious that this is
the method on which we base all our real beliefs and that on this,
above all, we base our belief in evolution. Of the thousands of
brilliant and elegant persons like ourselves who believe roughly in
the Darwinian doctrine, how many are there who know which fossil
or skeleton, which parrot's tail or which cuttle-fish's stomach,
is really believed to be the conclusive example and absolute datum
of natural selection? We know scarcely anything of the Darwinian
facts that lead to conversion. What we know is much more important: the Darwinian facts that come after conversion. What we
know, to use a higher language, are the fruits of the spirit. We
know that with this idea once inside our heads a million things
become transparent as if a lamp were lit behind them: we see the
thing in the dog in the street, in the pear on the wall, in the book
of history we are reading, in the baby in the perambulator and in
the last news from Borneo. And the fulfilments pour in upon us
in so natural and continual a cataract that at last is reached that
paradox of the condition which is called belief. We have seen so
many evidences of the theory that we have forgotten them all. The
theory is so clear to us that we can scarcely even defend it. If we
walked up to the nearest rationalist we know and asked him to
prove evolution, he would be dazed, like a man asked to defend
justice.

Now it ought to be clearly stated at this stage of philosophical development that it is most emphatically by this method of the successful hypothesis, of the theory that justifies itself, that so large a number of the young in this generation have returned to a certain doctrine of the spiritual. What this doctrine is it may be right to state as baldly and as briefly as possible; it is the view that the world, closely examined, does point with an extreme suggestiveness to the existence of a spiritual world, of a world of agencies not apparently produced by matter, capable to some extent of controlling and inspiring, capable to some extent of being known. It ought, I say, to be plainly stated that numbers of us have returned to this belief; and that we have returned to it, not because of this argument or that argument, but because the theory, when it is adopted, works out everywhere; because the coat, when it is tried on, fits in every crease. It ought to be stated because the old rationalists are rightly indignant with us, in so far as they fancy that we base such a tremendous doctrine on a few desperate quibbles; in so far as they fancy, as they do, that we are hanging on to religion by sticks and straws. . . . The return to the spiritual theory rests on none of these things. It rests, like the movement towards evolution, on the fact that the thing works out. We put on the theory like a magic hat and history becomes translucent like a house of glass.

Let us begin at the beginning. A startling and sensational event occurred recently; I allude to the emergence of the creature called man. It is a recent event, cosmically considered; it is, comparatively speaking, only a little too old to have been headlined in the evening papers. The newness, suddenness and utter uniqueness of the rise of man reminds one of Japan in the East; only it is more so. . . . There may be a hundred explanations of this. No sane man would say that it involved a spiritual deduction. But it fits in with it, and fits in with it very well, to suppose that there is another atmosphere of life besides the animal and that this spiritual world irrupted in some way into that creature at the moment. The phenomenon does not prove Religion, but religion explains the Phenomenon. The Phenomenon is quite as solitary as the Incarnation. It can be explained by saying that in a sense it was the Incarnation. Then we go on. There is one thing which the whole human race, without any exception at all, attests. From the dimmest ages and lands, wherever the seed of man is found, it declares this – that such an irruption did take place in the beginning, that they or their fathers have had dealings with a darker or more wonderful being. If human evidence means anything at all, this is perhaps the only thing on which we have overwhelming evidence.

We have nearly overwhelming human witness to the necessity of morality; we have quite overwhelming human witness to the reality of the spiritual life. We are ready enough to quote the evidence of all mankind in support of police regulations or the data of ethics; but we think mankind must be talking nonsense when, with one universal shout it cries out to this thing which is older than sin. That Marcus Aurelius and the Red Indians, that Hindu sages and Italian brigands and Mr Spurgeon and Sir William Crookes should all by various roads come to this conclusion, this is an important thing. A more important thing still is that this belief in spirit, so far from being a morbid thing, is held by almost all people who are physically strong and live in the open air. Powerful peasants and farmers six feet high all believe in fairies. Rationalism is a disease of the towns, like the housing problem. All this is, of course, only suggestive, but it is very suggestive. The Phenomenon does not prove Religion; but Religion explains the Phenomenon. ... We have not returned to the spiritual theory because of this or that triviality – because of a justification of the Fourth Gospel or a rap on the table. We have returned to it because, by the rejection of rationalism, the world becomes suddenly rational.

Daily News, March 14th, 1903

*   *   *

THE NECESSITY OF LUXURY

The great number of abuses peculiar to our present social state work back to that one great heresy which is the perversion of Darwin; I mean the heresy that man is an animal first and a spirit afterwards. The truth is that man is an animal and a spirit simultaneously, and his spiritual life is no more a luxury than his physical; except in the sense that he cannot rationally explain why he denies either of them. A humane and civilized happiness is one of man's needs, not merely one of his pleasures. Luxury is itself a necessity. Man does not live by bread alone but, at the very lowest level of thought, by bread and butter. All arguments about the treatment of the poor which are based on the idea that we can make them first contented animals and then go on to their souls, are false down to the root. By giving a man just enough air, just enough oatmeal, just enough exercise, just enough cocoa, you cannot make him a contented beast; but only a discontented man. . . . We shall never really get any further with our plans for the relief of distress until we have sufficient humility and sense of humour to leave off talking about what people need and bestow more attention on what they want.

The Open Review, July, 1906

*   *   *

THE CLUB

Mankind is not a tribe of animals to which we owe compassion. Mankind is a club to which we owe our subscription.

Daily News, April 10th, 1906

*   *   *

THE BIG THING AND THE SMALL

Sanity does not consist in seeing things; madmen see things more clearly than other people. Sanity consists in seeing the big things big and the small things small. A man can have this sense of proportion even if he is wrong. . . . Here is one case. Human society is the big and certain thing; pre-human evolution is the small and fanciful thing. To talk of 'humanity's' place in evolution is to be foolish and topsy-turvy. We do not know there was any evolution in the sense that we know that there is humanity. Some men hold that they are the children of apes; some that they are the children of Adam or of Wrath or of Mumbo-Jumbo.

These are creeds. But all men know that they are men; all men know that they belong to a positive human society, with rules of justice and mercy, and that they cannot even conceive themselves belonging to anything else. We belong to a club which is so old that nobody knows anything about its origin. We only know that in this club alone we can get our meals; in this club alone we can meet our friends; in this club alone we can sleep or argue or organize or pray. This club holds endless debates about everything – stars, boots, biology, sacraments, Alps, origins. Among the many minor things our human club discusses (for the fun of the thing) is how the club itself arose. The question is all the more interesting because nobody can answer it; the origins are in the fog of the utterly forgotten. Still, it is amusing to guess, and this guess or that guess is fashionable at any given time. At one time the club accepts the view that it was founded by a Mr Adam. At another time it records a vote that it was probably an affiliated branch of the Monkey's Club. But these discussions of the forgotten origins are meant to amuse the club. No one ever dreamt of their being allowed to destroy it. Yet they would certainly destroy the Human Club if once they meant that we were to be rude to the members or stingy to the waiters. This is the strongest instance I know of the big thing against the small; that Humanity is the huge house that I live in, while Evolution is the small but interesting animal which has quite recently asked to be domesticated in it.

Daily News, September 19th, 1908

* * *

'Working Out the Brute'

The worst result of popular evolutionism has been this. It has substituted the Beast for the Devil. It has made us think that our enemy is what they call our 'lower nature', which means our mere lusts and appetites, things entirely innocent in themselves. The most typical moderns have joined in this. Tennyson, for instance, spoke of moral improvement as 'moving upward, working out the brute'. But was he right? Why should we work out the brute? I no more desire, as such, to work out the brute from myself than to work out the brute from between the shafts of a hansom cab. The brute in me and the brute in the cab must both be kept in order. The brute in me and the brute in the cab have both very obvious uses. The thing that is wrong in us is not, as evolutionists say, the brute. The thing wrong in us is the devil, the austere, intellectual virgin devil of the medieval story. He will suffer for evil. He will perform heroic acts for evil . . .

Pigs are not corrupted with the Higher Imperialism. Tigers have no spiritual pride. Whales never sneer. Crocodiles are not (despite a pleasing legend) in the least hypocritical. On examining their exterior, it is difficult to understand why anyone ever gave them credit for so vivacious and ingenious a quality. The worst sins of all are the purely human sins. You may move upwards, working out the brute, and not work them out in the least. Nay, you may work them in. The less beastly you grow, the more bad you may grow.

Daily News, February 3rd, 1906

*　　*　　*

ORANGE PEEL AND THE FALL

This life of ours and the great pathway of history and civilization is a road entirely carpeted with orange peel. The obstacles are so numerous, the complications are so varied that we live, as it were, in an eternal crisis, in an immortal catastrophe. We are permanently in an exceptional state; nay, we are permanently in an unnatural state; this is what is meant by the Fall of Man. Even if we do not admit the Fall of Man, we must admit his continuous state of the staggers. The apple that Eve ate was an orange; and its peel has ever since strewed the ways of the world.

The Bystander, May 11th, 1904

*　　*　　*

ORIGINAL SIN

The true doctrine of original sin may be stated in a million ways, like every very central and solid truth. You may put it this way: that moral health is not a thing which will fulfil itself automatically in any complete man like physical health. Or this way: that we all start in a state of war. Or this way: that everything in a cabbage is trying to make a good cabbage, whereas everything in a man is not trying to make what we call a good man. Or this way: that virtue is a creditable thing and not merely, like the greenness of a cabbage, an admirable thing.

Daily News, September 2nd, 1905

*   *   *

THE OUTLINE OF THE FALL

Whether or no the garden was an allegory, the truth itself can be very well allegorized as a garden. And the point of it is that Man, whatever else he is, is certainly not merely one of the plants of the garden that has plucked its roots out of the soil and walked about with them like legs, or, on the principle of a double dahlia, has grown duplicate eyes and ears. He is something else, something strange and solitary, and more like the statue that was once the god of the garden; but the statue has fallen from its pedestal and lies broken among the plants and weeds. This conception has nothing to do with materialism as it refers to materials. The image might be made of wood; the wood might have come from the garden; the sculptor presumably might, and probably did, allow for the growth and grain of the wood in what he carved and expressed. But my fable fixes the two truths of the truer Scripture. The first is that the wood was graven or stamped with an image, deliberately and from outside; in this case the image of God. The second is that this image has been damaged and defaced so that it is now both better and worse than the mere plants in the garden which are perfect according to their own plan. There is room for any amount of speculation about the history of the tree before it was turned into an image; there is room for any amount of doubt and mystery about what really happened when it was turned into an image; there is room for any amount of hope and imagination about what it will look like when it is really mended and made into the perfect statue we have never seen. But it has the two fixed points, that man was uplifted at the first and fell; and to answer it by saying 'Where is the Garden of Eden?' is like answering a philosophical Buddhist by saying 'When were you last a donkey?'

The Fall is a view of life. It is not only the only enlightening but the only encouraging view of life. It holds, as against the only real alternative philosophies, those of the Buddhist or the Pessimist or the Promethean, that we have misused a good world and not merely been entrapped into a bad one. It refers evil back to the wrong use of the will and thus declares that it can eventually be righted by the right use of the will. Every other creed except that one is some form of surrender to fate. A man who holds this view of life will find it giving light on a thousand things on which mere evolutionary ethics have not a word to say. For instance, on the colossal contrast between the completeness of man's machines and the continued corruption of his motives; on the fact that no social progress really seems to leave self behind; on the fact that the first and not the last men of any school or revolution are generally the best and purest, as William Penn was better than a Quaker millionaire or Washington better than an American oil magnate; on that proverb which says 'The price of liberty is eternal vigilance', which is only what the theologians say of every other virtue and is itself only a way of stating the truth of original sin; on those extremes of good and evil by which man exceeds all the animals by the measure of heaven and hell; on that sublime sense of loss that is in the very sound of all great poetry, and nowhere more than in the poetry of pagans and sceptics – 'We look before and after and pine for what is not'; which cries against all prigs and progressives out of the very depths and abysses of the broken heart of man that happiness is not only a hope but also in some strange manner a memory; and that we are all kings in exile.

G. K.'s Weekly, September 25th, 1926

* * *

NEUROSIS

According to [a modern critic], it is morbid to confess your sins. I should say that the morbid thing is not to confess them. The morbid thing is to conceal your sins and let them eat your heart out, which is the happy state of most people in highly civilized communities.

Daily News, January 18th, 1908

*   *   *

THE BATTLE

The true secret and hope of human life is something much more dark and beautiful than it would be if suffering were a mark of sin. A mere scheme of rewards and punishments would be something much meaner and more mechanical than this exasperating and inspiring life of ours. An automatic scheme of 'Karma' or 'reaping what we sow' would be just as gross and material as sowing beans or reaping barley. It might satisfy mechanicians or monists or theosophists or cautious financiers, but not brave men. It is no paradox to say that the one thing that would make suffering intolerable would be the thought that it was systematically inflicted upon sinners. The one thing that would make our agony infamous would be the idea that it was deserved. On the other hand, the doctrine which makes it most endurable is exactly the opposite doctrine, that life is a battle in which the best put their bodies in the front, in which God sends only his holiest into the hail of the arrows of hell. In the book of Job is foreshadowed that better doctrine, full of a dark chivalry, that he that bore the worst that man can suffer was the best that bore the form of man.

The Speaker, September 9th, 1905

*   *   *

THE DECORATION

The Book of Job is better worth hearing than any modern philosophical conversation in the whole modern philosophical world. It is more philosophical. It is much more witty and humorous. It is, as that word is really meant, much more modern. From it the modern Agnostic may for the first time learn Agnosticism: a sane and sacred and manly ignorance. From it the modern Christian may with astonishment learn Christianity; learn, that is, that suffering may be a strange honour and not a vulgar punishment; that the King may be conferring a decoration when he pins the man on the cross, as much as when he pins the cross on the man.

Illustrated London News, February 10th, 1906

*　　　*　　　*

SURPRISE

Of one thing I am certain, that the age needs, first and foremost to be startled; to be taught the nature of wonder.

Black and White, February 14th, 1903

*　　　*　　　*

THE PHILOSOPHY OF PUMPKINS

There is no philosophical case against miracles. There are such things as the laws of Nature, rationally speaking. What everybody knows is this only, that there is repetition in nature. What everybody knows is that pumpkins produce pumpkins. What nobody knows is why they should not produce elephants and giraffes.

The question of miracles is merely this. Do you know why a pumpkin goes on being a pumpkin? If you do not, you cannot possibly tell whether a pumpkin could turn into a coach or couldn't. That is all.

All the other scientific expressions you are in the habit of using at breakfast are words and winds. You say, 'It is a law of nature that pumpkins should remain pumpkins'. That only means that pumpkins generally do remain pumpkins, which is obvious; it does not say why. You say, 'Experience is against it'. That only means, 'I have known many pumpkins intimately and none of them turned into coaches'. . . .

What Christianity says is merely this – that this repetition in Nature has its origin, not in a thing resembling a law, but in a thing resembling a will. Of course its phrase of a Heavenly Father is drawn from an earthly father. Quite equally [the] phrase of a universal law is a metaphor from an Act of Parliament. But

Christianity holds that the world and its repetition came by will or love, as children are begotten by a father, and therefore that other and different things might come by it. Briefly, it believes that a God who could do anything so extraordinary as making pumpkins go on being pumpkins is, like the prophet Habakkuk, *capable de tout*. If you do not think it extraordinary that a pumpkin is always a pumpkin, think again. You have not yet even begun philosophy. You have not even seen a pumpkin.

Daily News, September 2nd, 1905

* * *

'IN THE BEGINNING'

What is right with the world is the world. In fact, nearly everything else is wrong with it. This is that great truth in the tremendous tale of Creation, a truth that our people must remember or perish. It is at the *beginning* that things are good, and not (as the more pallid progressives say) only at the end. The primordial things – existence, energy, fruition – are good so far as they go. You cannot have evil life, though you can have notorious evil livers. Manhood and womanhood are good things, though men and women are often perfectly pestilent. You can use poppies to drug people, or birch trees to beat them, or stones to make an idol, or corn to make a corner; but it remains true that, in the abstract, before you have done anything, each of these four things is in strict truth a glory, a beneficent speciality and variety. We do praise the Lord that there are birch trees growing amongst the rocks and poppies amongst the corn; we do praise the Lord, even if we do not believe in Him. We do admire and applaud the *project* of a world, just as if we had been called to council in the primal darkness and seen the first starry plan of the skies. We are, as a matter of fact, far more certain that this life of ours is a magnificent and amazing enterprise than we are that it will succeed. ...

I am much more sure that everything is good at the beginning than I am that everything will be good at the end. ... That all this frame of things, this flesh, these stones, are good things, of that I am more brutally certain than I can say. But as for what will happen to them, that is to take a step into dogma and prophecy. I speak here, of course, solely of my personal feelings, not even of my reasoned creed. But on my instincts alone I should have no notion what would ultimately happen to this material world I think so magnificent. I am an agnostic, like most people with a positive theology. But I do affirm, with the full weight of sincerity, that trees and flowers are good at the beginning, whatever happens to them at the end; that human lives were good at the beginning, whatever happens to them in the end. The ordinary modern progressive position is that this is a bad universe, but will certainly get better. I say it is certainly a good universe, even if it gets worse. I say that these trees and flowers, stars and sexes, are primarily, not merely ultimately, good. In the Beginning the power beyond words created heaven and earth. In the Beginning He looked on them and saw that they were good.

All this unavoidable theory (for theory is always unavoidable) may be popularly pulled together thus. We are to regard existence as a raid or great adventure; it is to be judged, therefore, not by what calamities it encounters, but by what flag it follows and what high town it assaults. The most dangerous thing in the world is to be alive; one is always in danger of one's life. But anyone who shrinks from this is a traitor to the great scheme and experiment of being.

T. P.'s Weekly, Christmas Number, 1910

*　　*　　*

THE SAGE

If we test the matter by strict originality of outlook, George Macdonald was one of the three or four greatest men of nineteenth-century Britain. He does not in the ordinary sense occupy that position, because his art, though highly individual and fanciful, does not reach the level of his thought and passion. In the matter of expression, indeed, he suffered from his originality in a way that is more common than people realize. A man with a view of his own often cannot convey it to others, not because he does not understand his own view, but because he does not understand theirs. .... Hence arises a peculiar quality which may be noticed in the works of almost every man with a novel point of view; I mean, a tendency to become for a time unaccountably weak and obvious, to labour the simplest pieces of sentiment, to write pages of platitude. This, as I say, exists *par excellence* in the original men. It was so with Dickens. It was so with Victor Hugo. It was so with Ruskin. It was so with Thackeray. It was most assuredly so with George Macdonald. But those bursts of mysterious dullness or mysterious feebleness are, as above suggested, the direct product of the writer's bold independence and intense originality. He is so independent of conventions that he becomes conventional by accident. He is so unconscious of the beaten track that he even walks in it.

To appreciate properly men like Macdonald, it is necessary to remember a type of man who is a pillar of simple societies, but whom complex societies tend to turn into something else. I mean the sage, the sayer of things. He is not the poet, for he does not sing; he is not the prose writer, for generally he cannot write. The things he produces form an artistic class by themselves; they are *logia* or great passionate maxims, the proverbs of philosophy. Confucius was a man of this kind, and the real Socrates and most of the founders of the great religions. But in our modern and respectable and highly specialized world we do not like to leave an old gentleman loose about the streets merely saying things. The man who is naturally and spiritually of this type is in our time forced to pretend to be something else, a minor poet or a novelist or some sad kind of political reformer.

For instance, a man in the modern world who belonged naturally to this class in a pre-eminent degree was Walt Whitman. Critics fuss themselves for ever about whether he was a poet or a prose writer. As a matter of fact, he was neither a poet nor a prose writer; he was a sayer of great things. He excelled in a sort of primeval epigram. 'I do not give lectures or a little charity; when I give, I give myself.' 'Do we find life so well provided for and think that death is not equally well provided for?' These have all the characteristics of the logia on which were founded the larger faiths of mankind. And Whitman would have much preferred to have shouted them in the streets, like John the Baptist or Mahomet, to being obliged to include them in what he was obliged to call poems.

George Macdonald was in the same way not a born writer; he was a born maker of spontaneous texts. He also would have very much preferred to walk about the streets of some Greek or eastern village with a long white beard, simply saying what he had to say. But just as Whitman had to label his tracts of truth poetry, Macdonald labelled his novels. There are some exceptions, but in the main it is true to say that we only remember his novels, as we only remember Whitman's poetry, by certain bursts of an astonishing sagacity, often uttered in five words. Anyone who has read Macdonald's novels will remember a sort of celestial wit in some of the dialogues, retorts that seem really like thunderbolts from heaven. . . . For him the secret of the Cosmos was a secret, because it was too good to tell. The stars and all things in his world tingled with the tension of that painful pleasure of the soul. For him the pity of God was so positive as to be a definite passion like thirst; it was a fierce tenderness; he was never tired of saying that his God was a consuming fire.

Daily News, September 23rd, 1905

*   *   *

INTIMATIONS

Matthew Arnold did not often say a thoroughly silly thing, but he did when he criticized Wordsworth for talking of the wonderland of childhood and objected that a man of thirty had a better appreciation of landscape, as of course he has in the sense of landscape gardening. But the white light which Wordsworth meant was not in the sky the child looked at, but in the child. He happened to be a country child; but it was really only a geographical accident that it was meadow, grove and stream, and not post, pavement and policeman that were apparelled in celestial light, the glory and freshness of a dream. Nor is it the mere memory of vigour and adventure which really is stronger at sixteen than at six; it is quite a different sensation. And to this day I cannot see certain things such as a white horse or wood painted white, without a pang of pleasure going through me stronger than sex or the fear of death. And unlike sex and death, it does not concentrate; for an instant, like a lost lightning flash, it has spread over the whole world, full of too many wonders to be wondered at.

Here enters the psychological educationist with his subconsciousness and his first impressions, to remark shrewdly, 'This is because somebody in your childhood gave you a wooden horse or painted it white for you'. To which I reply respectfully, 'Yes, fool, yes. Admirable and astonishing idiot, quite so. But has it ever occurred to you to ask why a pot of paint and a piece of wood should blaze with divine beauty to anybody at any time; or why they should do it to a child of four any more than to a man of forty? When you have retired for a few years to reflect on the point, we will resume this conversation.'

The New Witness, June 17th, 1921

*　　*　　*

THE LITTLE THINGS

Sir Thomas Browne was an exalted mystic [whose mysticism] owed much to his literary style. Style, in his sense, did not merely mean sound, but an attempt to give some twist of wit or symbolism to every clause or parenthesis; when he went over his work again, he did not merely polish brass, he fitted in gold. This habit of working with a magnifying glass, this turning and twisting of minor words, is the true parent of mysticism; for the mystic is not a man who reverences large things so much as a man who reverences small ones, who reduces himself to a point, without parts or magnitude, so that to him the grass is really a forest and the grasshopper a dragon. Little things please great minds.

The Speaker, December 15th, 1900

*　　*　　*

'MERE PARADOX'

The simplest and commonest of all the causes which lead to the charge of 'mere paradox' being slung about as it is, is one fundamental assumption. Everybody takes it for granted that universal and ordinary arrangements, historic institutions, daily habits are reasonable. They are good, they are sensible, they are holy and splendid often enough, but they are not reasonable. They are themselves paradoxes; paradox is built into the very foundations of human affairs.

Black and White, February 14th, 1903

* * *

THE HIPPOPOTAMUS AND THE CROCODILE

There is one central conception of the book of Job which literally makes it immortal, which will make it survive our modern time and our modern philosophies, as it has survived many better times and many better philosophies. That is the conception that the universe, if it is to be admired, is to be admired for its strangeness and not for its rationality, for its splendid unreason and not for its reason. Job's friends attempt to comfort him with philosophical optimism, like the intellectuals of the eighteenth century. Job tries to comfort himself with philosophical pessimism, like the intellectuals of the nineteenth century. But God comforts Job with indecipherable mystery, and for the first time Job is comforted. Eliphaz gives one answer, Job gives another answer, and the question still remains an open wound. God simply refuses to answer, and somehow the question is answered. Job flings at God one riddle, God flings back at Job a hundred riddles, and Job is at peace. He is comforted with conundrums. For the grand and enduring idea in the poem, as suggested above, is that if we are to be reconciled to this great cosmic experience, it must be as something divinely strange and divinely violent, a quest or a conspiracy or some sacred joke. The last chapters of the colossal monologue of the Almighty are devoted, in a style superficially queer enough, to the detailed description of two monsters. Behemoth and Leviathan may or may not be the hippopotamus and the crocodile. But whatever they are, they are evidently embodiments of the enormous absurdity of nature. They typify that cosmic trait which anyone may see in the Zoological Gardens, the folly of the Lord which is wisdom. And in connection with one of them, God is made to utter a splendid satire upon the prim and orderly piety of the vulgar optimist. 'Wilt thou play with him as with a bird? Wilt thou bind him for thy maidens?' That is the main message of the book of Job. Whatever this cosmic monster may be, a good animal or a bad animal, he is at least a wild animal and not a tame animal. It is a wild world and not a tame world.

The Speaker, September 9th, 1905

*　　　*　　　*

CHANGE AND DECAY

All this talk about optimism and pessimism is itself a dismal fall from the old talk about right and wrong. Our fathers said that a nation had sinned and suffered, like a man. We say it has decayed, like a cheese.

Illustrated London News, July 10th, 1920

*　　　*　　　*

THE ENEMIES OF JOY

It is a blunder to imagine, as many do, that those who agree with me wish to make every man a Robinson Crusoe, making all his own clothes and living only for himself. As a fact, the peasant, though he has much of the handy universality of Robinson Crusoe, can never be content with the solitude of Robinson Crusoe. A peasant lives in a peasantry and not on a desert island. He is by nature as ready for co-operation as he is resolute against communism. Still, there is something symbolic in the figure of Robinson Crusoe and especially in its fascination of the innocent imagination of the most creative period of childhood. Why is it that a child is delighted with the idea of Robinson Crusoe, complete with his gun and umbrella, his goat and parrot, his axe and antiquated sword? It is precisely because he is complete and also compact; that he has a limited number of things but these things immediately at hand and directly under his control. It is equally or perhaps even more because these things have been barely snatched from the bottomless peril of shipwreck and the dark infinity of the sea. That is the right view of the good things of life; we should possess them directly, but we should possess them thriftily and above all, we should possess them thankfully. They and we have been saved by God out of the sea of nothing and the night that was before the world.

Now in the course of my life I have seen this compact conception, symbolized by Robinson Crusoe in the children's books, attacked by two opposite enemies, but with equal enmity. The old enemy called itself pessimism; the new enemy calls itself Progress and Optimism; but both invade the desert island with the destructive frenzy of the cannibals. The old fashion took the form of pointing out how very desert was the desert island, how very dull was the life of Crusoe and how very insignificant, intrinsically considered, was each of the pleasures that remained to him. What was a parrot but a proverb for something that repeated itself over and over again? What is the use of a goat – except to play the goat? What is an umbrella, said one sad philosopher, but something which can only be opened when it is shut and then shut when it is open? He always implied that life was dreary on a desert island only because it would be dreary anywhere else. For him England was a desert island; for him the coming of Friday would indeed have marked a day of ill luck. He was the sort of pessimist who curses both the solitude and the intruder on the solitude. This sort of sweeping negation moved me in my youth to a romantic revolt and a wild enthusiasm for the poetry of umbrellas. I shocked some critics by a sympathy with playing the goat; others still more by a sympathy with playing with the gun. But while I valued these things, I valued them most of all because they were few and clear, and picked out in conspicuous colours against the desolation of the destructive sea.

I have since seen something which claims to be the contrary philosophy, but for me is the same heresy. The world has improved on the one parrot by becoming a screaming parrot-house. It has improved on the faithful goat by filling the island with herds and herds of goats that have not a goatherd. I have seen it proclaimed that Crusoe's umbrella will be universally popular if it is expanded into the awning of a universal pavilion, placarded with advertisements of pills or pictures of mixed bathing. I have seen even the gun excused if it is a big enough gun manufactured by a big enough firm; and the axe counted innocent if it is what we call 'an axe to grind'. Yet all this paradise of perfect happiness fails to lift my heart or reawaken the faintest hint of that first romantic interest in Robinson Crusoe. And the reason is that this sort of sweeping generalization, quite as much as the old sweeping negation, implies a contempt for the few original facts of the story which alone made it interesting. The optimist, as much as the pessimist, asks what is the good of one shabby old umbrella or one shaggy old goat. That is, he commits the star-blasting blasphemy of depreciating the things that the man has actually saved from the wreck. The sin of the optimist is that he does not recognize the wreck; as the sin of the pessimist is that he does not recognize the rescue.

Now I am fundamentally convinced that the only thing worth calling a thrill (to use the juvenile jargon of today) is the thought that comes in the transition from the wreck to the rescue. It belongs to a class of thoughts which are best represented by thanks, but which are approximately represented by an imaginative realization of what is and what might have been. It exists on an edge, like the edge of the land and sea; and is unknown to the suicide who feels himself a castaway in mid-ocean and to the self-satisfied settler who has travelled so far inland as to forget the bright fear or shining mystery of the sea. All real happiness I have ever had or have ever seen anybody else having had something in it of that first unfamiliarity and shyness; and it is lost by the pride of possession as by the pride of refusal. Therefore those who say they are running after the thrill are in reality running away from the thrill. They are leaving it further and further behind, the more they accumulate more luxuries than they can enjoy or combine more pleasures than they can distinguish.

G. K.'s Weekly, October 11th, 1930

*　　　*　　　*

AUTOBIOGRAPHY

The heresies that have attacked human happiness in my time
have all been variations of either presumption or despair; which in
the controversies of modern culture are called optimism and pessimism. And if I wanted to write an autobiography in a sentence
(and I hope I shall never write a longer one), I should say that my
literary life has lasted from a time when men were losing happiness by despair to a time when they are losing it by presumption.

Blackfriars, January, 1923

*   *   *

LIFE AND LIBERTY

I was brought up in a fairly typical middle-class English family.

My father had been prosperous in business and he had felt that
something more than business was needed to square oneself with
the universe.

He was a Unitarian.

There was not a Unitarian tradition in the family. But that was
the mode of the age.

And I think that from my very junior youth I felt that something more was needed.

I don't think that I myself have ever changed.

From the beginning I think I was staggered by the stupendous
marvel of existence – by the miracle of sunlight coming through a
window, by the miracle of people walking on legs through the
streets, by the miracle of people talking to each other.

This marvel fascinated me, as it does today.

And I said to myself – or I might have said to myself – well,
is not that enough? And Echo might have answered:

'Yes, it is enough. If you see it. And if you will always see it.'

Rather a large mouthful for Echo! But as a matter of fact, that
is what Echo said.

Which brings me to what was an important event in my life,
though, as I say, thinking led up to it.

I got hold of *Leaves of Grass* by Walt Whitman. I called it then a revelation. It put in black and white the things I had always known. The glory and magic of God's universe – the shows of night and day and 'in the midst, God's beautiful right hand'.

Well, very soon I found that those who imitated Whitman's irregular lines missed out the magic of the universe and were definitely antagonistic to God's beautiful right hand. That was disturbing. God was all right, the universe was all right, Whitman was all right. But something had gone wrong.

Then again, as a very young fellow, I was a Socialist.

I think I have always hated the idea of things being done from a centre.

I hated bureaucracy.

But they told me that if I wanted to get rid of the manifold iniquities of aggressive capital, of interest, I must get rid of private property.

And so I believed them.

Although what I really believed in was the sort of thing that William Morris pictures, with every craftsman running his own show.

Perhaps the catastrophic event – if you want one – was the South African War.

There I saw something which seemed to me to be the meanest kind of financial grab, supported by fine sincere fellows like Stopford Brooke (at whose feet I had sat as a child), York Powell and the Fabians – apparently merely because the British Empire was big and the Transvaal Republic was little.

That stirred me up. Why did all these fine men and women go wrong?

Again, I have always believed in Liberty.

But I noticed that all those who said they believed in Liberty and nothing else, proceeded at once to shackle themselves.

Look at the old S.D.F.-ers. Splendid fellows like Hyndman and Bax!

But what they did was to adopt an economic creed (which the Russians hold today) that everything that happens must happen – that, in fact, nobody can be free. It seemed a poor way to use your freedom.

And, mark you, I have noticed that the modern idea of freedom seems to be that you are not to be allowed to bring up your family as you choose, that you are not to be allowed to marry as you choose, that you are not to be allowed to drink as you choose.

I soon came to realize that liberty was a more complicated thing than I had imagined and that it seemed to need somebody (perhaps God) standing outside human life as an arbiter.

One of the things that have made a difference to me is owning my own place in the country. I was born and bred a Cockney. I was altogether urban. And then I moved into the country and bought a field. My own field! My very own!

And then I built a studio on it. My very own studio. I could enact my own (or my wife's) plays in that studio and whoever said me nay could go to blazes. And then the house grew on to the studio.

And now I am proud to say that I can grow in my garden enough to keep my family alive if our toppling system of credit went to pieces and our great cities were famine-stricken.

Yes, I have learnt the meaning of ownership. I know what liberty really means.

But I cannot leave out God. For I have seen so many things go wrong when they left out God.

Liberty became licence – desperate, sordid licence – or became sheer slavery, property became monopoly. And the miracle of everyday life became of no account at all.

And so I, who began as a Protestant, remain one as a Catholic – a Protestant against the destruction of all the material, simple things.

I have not changed. God made me; and here I am.

Socialism failed me and I have turned my back on that because it was not social.

Protestantism failed me and I have turned my back on that because it did not protest.

These things endure: life and liberty and the boundless magic of night and day – and what comes after.

Daily Sketch, May 14th, 1931

(*This passage was obviously not written by Chesterton. It is presumably a write-up of an interview with him but is worth re-printing for its intrinsic interest.*)

*   *   *

THE LESSON

Pessimism is a thing which is learnt from books, as sorrow is a thing learnt from life. Sorrow can never be pessimistic, for it is founded upon the value of things.

Daily News, June 13th, 1903

*   *   *

THE TRUE CRITIC

Optimism is said to be unpopular just at present, and optimism in criticism lies under a specially withering disdain. But for all that, criticism will have to become more optimistic or lose altogether its hold upon the future. The only bad thing about criticism is its name. It is derived from a word signifying a criminal judge, and hitherto it has been supposed in consequence that criticism has to do with literary crimes. The favourable judgement of the critic has always been, in the ordinary opinion, to acquit a man of sin, not to convict him of a merit. If criticism were in a sound state, it would have discovered some one epithet to express the value of Coleridge instead of half a hundred epithets to express the use-lessness of Marie Corelli.

Optimism, or the utmost possible praise of all things, ought to be the keynote of criticism. It may appear to be an audacious asser-tion, but it may be tested by one very large and simple process. Compare the reality of a man's criticism when praising anything with its reality when excluding anything, and we shall all feel how much more often we agree with the former than with the latter. ... In praising great men we cheerfully agree to a superlative, but we emphatically decline a comparative. We come very near to the optimism of that universal superlative which in the morning of the world declared all things to be very good.

One of the results of this fact is that when a critic is really large-minded and really sympathetic and comprehensive, and really has hold of a guiding and enlightening idea, he should

173

still watch with the greatest suspicion his own limitations and rejections. His praise will almost certainly be sound; his blame should always remain to his own mind a little dubious.

The Speaker, May 3rd, 1902

* * *

FAIRY TALES

Fairy tales are the only true accounts that man has ever given of his destiny. 'Jack the Giant-Killer' is the embodiment of the first of the three great paradoxes by which men live. It is the paradox of Courage: the paradox which says, 'You must defy the thing that is terrifying; unless you are frightened, you are not brave.' 'Cinderella' is the embodiment of the second of the paradoxes by which men live: the paradox of Humility which says 'Look for the best in the thing, ignorant of its merit; he that abases himself shall be exalted'. And 'Beauty and the Beast' is the embodiment of the third of the paradoxes by which men live: the paradox of Faith – the absolutely necessary and wildly unreasonable maxim which says to every mother with a child or to every patriot with a country, 'You must love the thing first and make it lovable afterwards.'

The World, September 27th, 1904

* * *

THE ETHICS OF FAIRYLAND

Of all forms of literature, it seems to me, fairy tales give the truest picture of life. There may be errors in detail, but in a world so full of strange things they scarcely matter. Two-headed giants and beanstalks that climb up into the sky may not be true, but assuredly they are not too wonderful to be true. But the atmosphere of the fairy tale is astonishingly true to life. It deals with the silent witchery that lies in common things, corn and stones and apple trees and fire. It presents these, no doubt, as magic stones and magic apple trees, and if anyone will stare at them steadily in a field at twilight, he will find himself quite unable to assert that they are not magic.

174

Let me take one quite practical example of the truth of fairy tales. In these stories success is made to depend upon a number of small material objects and observances; life is a chain of talismans. If a man touches three trees in passing, he is safe; if he touches four, he is ruined. If the hero meets a miller without a beard, he is to answer none of his questions. If he plucks a red flower in a particular meadow, he will have power over the mighty kings of some distant city. Now this poetic sense of the decisiveness of some flying detail is a thousand times more genuine and practical than the pompous insistence on some moral or scientific law which is the basis of most realistic novels. None of us know when we have done something irrevocable. Our fate has been often decided by the twist of a road or the shape of a tree. Nay, it has often been decided by an omnibus or an advertisement, and there can therefore be little reason for denying that it is a magic omnibus or a magic advertisement.

The great truth and value of the fairy-tale view of life cannot be better conveyed than by saying that it chiefly arises from the entire absence of the supernatural in fairy tales. There is no miraculous department there, nothing conceived as outrageous or exceptional, nothing that recalls crystal-gazing and planchette. There is no trace or hint of that modern 'spiritual world' which implies that this world is not spiritual. In the fairy tales, portents are orderly and inevitable; they are part of the very texture of natural life. In a place so strange as this earth it is as natural to meet griffins and witches and three-headed dogs as to meet geese and oxen. This earth of ours is conceived as a place full of innumerable marvels ... The fairy-tale hero is impressed, doubtless, when the pumpkin turns into a coach or the castle soars into the air. But he is not impressed for the mean and stupid reason that he had thought the world was prosaic. Life for him is an illimitable sea of monsters. He is often astonished, but, if I may employ the phrase, he would be more astonished if he were not astonished.

It is a great mistake to imagine that fairy tales are either immoral or unmoral. They do not tally with the trivialities of every particular moral code, but in this respect they resemble all works of art. ... In them we see the great lines of elementary laws and ideals as we see them nowhere else. We learn first and foremost that all doors fly open to courage and to hope. We learn that the world is bound together in mysterious bonds of trust and compact and prevision, and that even green dragons keep their promises. We learn that nothing is wasted in the mills of the world, that a jewel thrown into the sea, a kindness to a stricken bird, an idle word to a ragged wayfarer, have in them some terrible value and are here bound up with the destiny of men. Nothing is more typical and recurrent in the ethics of the fairy tale than the great idea that nothing can be lost. . . . The world is ruled by a sublime parsimony; there is no such thing as a dustbin in the house of God.

This is one very characteristic moral of fairy tales, the idea of the indestructibility of an essence or an act. Another fully as common and even more essential is the great idea which lies at the heart of the story of 'Beauty and the Beast' and a hundred kindred tales; the idea that by loving a thing we make it beautiful. The fairy tale warns us to be on our guard against the disguises of things and to regard every ugly and repellent exterior with a hopeful and divine suspicion.

But all these massive fragments of primitive morality are secondary to the great moral spirit which is the very heart of the fairy tales. That spirit is the principle appearing and reappearing in a thousand folklore stories, that nothing can do a man harm unless he fears it. At no time in the history of civilization, perhaps, has there been so much need to recall the ethics of the ancient warfare of Jack against the Giant, of the small against the gigantic. Those who in our day express a peculiar sympathy with the weak in their struggle against the strong are often accused of indulging a hypersensitive humanitarianism unknown to the robuster ages of the world. The thing is a delusion. The sympathy for the weak against the strong speaks out of the oldest twilight; it is the very backbone of the most savage stories with which we have to deal in anthropology. For the fairy tale is only the history of man himself, at once the weakest and the strongest of the creatures.

The Speaker, October 12th, 1901

*   *   *

DIVINE IMMANENCE

It is evident that, though all things are divine, all things are limited. And among other divine things, man himself is limited. He has not the memory nor the imagination nor the vigilance nor the sheer physical health to realize the Godhead in every atom or object that passes under his hands. A person who never neglected any object: a man who burst into religious tears as he fastened a divine collar with an inspired collar-stud, and continued thus with everything he looked at, would go mad in five minutes; he would see God and die. The only things which man, a limited animal, can do in this matter, are two; first, he can believe (as an absolute thing of faith) that there is this divinity in things, whether he sees it or not; second, he can leave himself reasonably open to those sudden revelations whereby one or two of these things – a cloud, a man's face, a noise in the dark – may for some reason no one has ever been able to offer, capriciously reveal its divinity. . . .

I believe that every object is divine in a very definite and thorough sense. I believe, that is to say, that there is a great pressure of spiritual reality behind things as they seem, and of this view, as I have said continuously, the proof lies in the explanation it affords of countless human affairs. And I believe that the supreme instance and the supreme demonstration of it is this; that if a man, dismissing the Cosmos and all such trifles, looks steadily and with some special and passionate adoration at some one thing, that thing suddenly speaks to him. Divinity lurks not in the All, but in everything; and that, if it be true, is the explanation of a load of human chronicles, of a cataract of human testimony of all the religions, and all the wild tales of the world. . . . Providence desires its gifts received intensely and with humility and it is possible to look at one of them steadily and confidently until, with a great cry, it gives up its god.

Daily News, March 24th, 1903

* * *

A LOCAL HABITATION

It is not enough for a religion to include everything. It must include everything and something over. That is, it must include everything and include something as well. It must answer that deep and mysterious human demand for something as distinct from the demand for everything, even if the nature of that demand be too deep to be easily defined in logic. It will never cease to be described in poetry. We might almost say that all poetry is a description of it. Even when you have only natural religion, you will still have supernatural poetry. And it will be poetic because it is particular, not because it is general. The new priest may proclaim, 'The sea is God, the land is God and the sky is God; but yet there are not three Gods, but one God'. But even if the old priest be silenced, the old poet will always answer, 'God is in a cave; God is in a stable; God is disguised and hidden. I alone know where he is; he is herding the cattle of Admetus, he is pouring out the wine of Cana.' The new republic may make the philosophical declaration, 'We hold these truths to be self-evident, that all trees are evolved equal and endowed with the dignity of creative evolution.' But if in the silence that follows we overhear the poor nurse or the peasant mother telling fairy tales to the children, she will always be saying, 'And in the seventh garden beyond the seventh gate was the tree with the golden apples'; or 'They sailed and sailed until they came to an island, and on the island was a meadow, and in the meadow the tree of life' . . .

Now if this particularism always stubbornly recurs even in poetry, how can it be left out of philosophy? What is the *meaning* of this incurable itch to give to airy nothing, or still more airy everything, a local habitation and a name? Why is it always something at once odd and objective, a precious fruit or a flying cup or a buried key, that symbolizes the mystery of the world? Why should not the world symbolize the world? Why should not a sphere sufficiently symbolize universalism, so that the faithful might be found adoring a plum-pudding or a cannon-ball? Why should not a spiral sufficiently represent progress, and the pious bow down before a corkscrew? In practice we know that it would be impossible to dissociate a Christmas pudding from the sacramental specialism of Christmas; and the worship of the corkscrew, that hieratic serpent, would probably be traced to the mysteries of Dionysius. In a word, *why* are all mysteries concerned with the notion of finding a particular thing in a particular place? If we are to find the real meaning of every element in mythology, what is the real meaning of *that* element in it? I can see only one possible answer that satisfies the new more serious and sympathetic study of religion, even among sceptics, and that is that there really is something to which all these fancies are what forgeries are to a signature; that if the soul could be satisfied with the truth, it would find it a tale as particular, as positive and as personal; that the light which we follow first as a wide white star actually narrows as we draw nearer to it, till we find that the trailing meteor is something like a light in a window or a candle in a room.

New Witness, July 15th, 1921

* * *

SACRAMENT OR MAGIC

Whenever men really believe that they can get to the spiritual, they always employ the material. When the purpose is good, it is bread and wine; when the purpose is evil, it is eye of newt and toe of frog.

Illustrated London News, September 22nd, 1906

* * *

THE CONCRETE AND THE ABSTRACT

Thinkers of [a certain] school have a tendency to believe that the concrete is the symbol of the abstract. The truth, the truth at the root of all mysticism, is quite the other way. The abstract is the symbol of the concrete. This may possibly seem at first sight a paradox; but it is a purely transcendental truth. We see a green tree. It is the green tree that we cannot understand; it is the green tree which we fear; it is the green tree which we worship. Then, because there are so many green trees, so many men, so many elephants, so many butterflies, so many daisies, so many animalculae, we coin a general term 'Life'. And then the mystic comes and says that a green tree symbolizes life. It is not so. Life symbolizes a green tree. Just in so far as we get into the abstract, we get away from the reality, we get away from the mystery, we get away from the tree. And this is the reason that so many transcendental discourses are merely blank and tedious to us, because they have to do with Truth and Beauty and the Destiny of the Soul and all the great faint, jaded symbols of the reality. And this is why poetry is so interesting to us, because it has to do with skies, with woods, with battles, with temples, with women and with wine, with the ultimate miracles which no philosopher could create. The difference between the concrete and the abstract is the difference between the country and the town. God made the concrete, but man made the abstract. A truthful man is a miracle, but the truth is a commonplace.

The Speaker, May 31st, 1902

*   *   *

THE LIGHT AND THE HEAT

The Jews, with their wonderful instinct for practical religion, swore that he who looked upon Jehovah died; but in a large number of transcendental schools and sages the sentence of death has been commuted to a doom of gibbering idiocy. To the Buddhists was given a conception of God of extraordinary intellectual purity; but in growing familiar with the featureless splendour, they have lost their heads; they babble; they say that everything is nothing and nothing is everything, that black is white because white is black. We fancy that the frightful universal negatives at which they have at last arrived, are really little more than the final mental collapse of men trying always to find an abstraction big enough for all things. 'I have said what I understood not, things too great for me that I know not. I will put my hand upon my mouth.' Job was a wise man. ... Buddhism stands for a simplification of the mind and a reliance on the most indestructible ideas; Christianity stands for a simplification of the heart and a reliance on the most indestructible sentiments. The greater Christian insistence upon personal deity and immortality is not, we fancy, the cause so much as the effect of this essential trend towards an ancient passion and pathos as the power that most nearly rends the veil from the nature of things. Both creeds grope after the same secret sun, but Buddhism dreams of its light and Christianity of its heat. Buddhism seeks after God with the largest conception it can find, the all-producing and all-absorbing One; Christianity seeks after God with the most elementary passion it can find – the craving for a father, the hunger that is as old as the hills. It turns the whole cry of a lost universe into the cry of a lost child.

The Speaker, November 17th, 1900

*　　*　　*

A NOTE ON COMPARATIVE RELIGION

Christianity is not a religion; it is a Church. There may be a Moslem religion; but it would not come natural to anybody to talk about the Moslem Church. There may be a Buddhist religion; but nobody would call it the Buddhist Church. . . . I say that the very idea of a Catholic Church is *sui generis*, apart from claims to embody it. I am not now talking about the comparison with Christian heresies, but of the comparison with heathen religions. It does indeed illustrate the incongruous and incomparable assortment of rival religions that one of them does actually belong to this other category. One of the heathen religions really is a Christian heresy. The more we know of the great Moslem movement, the more we see that it was really a post-Christian revision, or subsequent simplification rather like the Arian movement. Of the other things that we call Eastern religions many existed before Christianity, and almost any might have existed without Christianity. I take it as certain that Islam would never have existed without Christianity. I take it to be as clear as that Calvinism or Lollardism or Lutheranism would never have existed without Christianity. Nor was the Moslem movement in the modern sense anti-Christian. It gave to Christ as high a moral position as is given Him by most Unitarians, and indeed a more supernatural status than is given by some Broad Churchmen. To do Mahomet justice, his main attack was against the idolatries of Asia. . . .

Now we might apply this principle of differentiation to each of the rival religions in turn. Each of them is not only in a different category from the Catholic Church, but in a different category from the others. Islam, if it is to go into a class at all, ought not to go into a class of Islam, Christianity, Confucianism and Brahminism, but rather into a class of Islam, Manicheeism, Pelagianism and Protestantism. In the same way, Buddha ought not really to go into a class of Buddha, Christ, Mahomet and the rest; but rather into some such class as Buddha, Pythagoras, Plato and so on. He belongs to that class of philosophical mystics for whom what we commonly call religion was really only symbolical, and the main matter was a metaphysical unification. He may have had some of the virtues of a saint, but he was in reality a sage. He may have been what we call an idealist; he was also something very like a pessimist. But anyhow he was not a Church and did not found a Church. To consider what he did found, we should have to go back to the foundations in Brahminism; and when we do so, we find that this in turn is not another variation of the same thing, but an utterly different sort of thing with variations of its own. It is rather an old popular mythology, like our own old pagan mythology. At the back of it Brahminism is probably nature-worship, and Buddhism is certainly the very opposite of nature-worship. It would be true to call it an iconoclasm directed to destroy the idol called nature.

Finally, it is fairly clear that Confucianism is not a religion, unless the English public-school system is a religion or the *Kultur* of imperial Germany was a religion. In a sense they may be so described, since everything rests on a conscious or unconscious religion, or negation of religion. But nobody would call any of them a Church; and nobody can compare them with a Church calling itself dogmatic and divine. All these disparate things, of which one is an imitation and another a doubt and another a book of etiquette, have nothing in common except that they are none of them Churches; and that they are all examples of the various things in which man might be expected to experiment in the absence of a Church....

It is a simple and historical fact about the Catholic Church that its character is as extraordinary as its claim. It is not merely the only thing that deserves a particular kind of service; it is the only thing that asks for it. It is quite possible to be a pagan and hate the Church; it is equally possible to be a pessimist and hate the universe. But there is one Church exactly as there is one universe; and no wise man will wander about looking for another.

Blackfriars, March, 1923

* * *

ASSIMILATION AND REJECTION

The instant it is said that we should take the good things from every atmosphere or system, an immediate question springs to the lips. But what about the bad things? ... A religion should not only be instinctively absorbent of whatever is consonant with its ideal; it should be instinctively resistant to anything that is against that ideal. Men look to a faith to purge them of all native poisons as well as to develop all native functions and pleasures. A Church should have drainage as well as ventilation. It should drive bad smells out as well as let good smells in; it should not only cast out devils, but keep them out.

Daily News, March 19th, 1910

* * *

THE WINTER FEAST

It is the greatest glory of the Christian tradition that it has incorporated so many Pagan traditions. But it is most glorious of all, to my mind, when they are popular traditions. And the best and most obvious example is the way in which Christianity did incorporate, in so far as it did incorporate, the old human and heathen conception of the Winter Feast....

There is a perfectly natural parallel between a religion that

defies the world and a ritual that defies the weather. Heathenism
in the sense of hedonism, the concentration of the mind on pure
pleasure as such, would chiefly concentrate on the conception of a
Summer Feast. But in winter even a rich man receives some faint
hint of the problem of a poor man; he may avoid being hungry,
but he cannot always avoid being cold. To choose that moment of
common freezing for the assertion of common fraternity is, in its
own intrinsic nature, a foreshadowing of what we call the Christian
idea. It involves the suggestion that joy comes from within and
not from without. It involves the suggestion that peril and the
potentiality of pain are themselves a ground for gratitude and
rejoicing. It involves the suggestion that even when we are merely
Pagans, we are not merely Pantheists. We are not merely nature
worshippers; because a man smiles when nature frowns. It has
always involved, under varying limitations in varying societies,
the idea of hospitality, especially hospitality to the stranger and
generally to the poor. Of course there are perfectly natural reasons
for wanting to drink wine or warm ourselves at the fire in winter;
but that is not an answer, except to those who have the ill-informed
prejudice that Christianity must be opposed to things merely
because they are natural. The point is in making a point of it; the
special interest is in the special occasion, in the fact that during the
Winter Feast, whether Pagan or Christian, there always was in
some degree the idea of extending the enjoyment to others, of passing round the wine or seating the wanderer by the hearth. It is
no controversial point against the Christians that they felt they
could take up and continue such traditions among the Pagans; it
only shows that the Christians knew a Christian thing when they
saw it.

The real history of Christmas is very relevant to the real crisis
of Christendom. We live in a terrible time of war and rumour of
war; with a barbaric danger of the real reaction that goes back,
not to the old form, but to the old formlessness. International
idealism in its effort to hold the world together in a peace that can
resist wars and revolutions, is admittedly weakened and often dis-
appointed. I should say simply that it does not go deep enough. Christianity could draw life out of the depths of Paganism; but mere

Modernism cannot draw on the depths of either. Charity is too much of a manufactured article and too little of a natural product. The League of Nations is too new to be natural. The modern materialistic humanitarianism is too young to be vigorous. If we really wish to make vivid the horrors of destruction and mere disciplined murder, we must see them more simply as attacks on the hearth and the human family. If we want to talk about poverty, we must talk about it as the hunger of a human being, a pain as positive as toothache; and not as the fall in wages or the failure of imports or even the lowering of the economic standard of living. We must say first of the beggar, not that there is insufficient housing accommodation but that he has nowhere to lay his head. We must say first of the human family, not that there are no jobs for them in the factory, but that there is no room for them in the inn. That is, we must talk of the human family in language as plain and practical and positive as that in which mystics used to talk of the Holy Family. We must learn again to use the naked words that describe a natural thing, and dispense for a moment with all those sociological polysyllables with which an artificial society has learned to talk of it as an artificial thing. Then we shall draw on the driving force of many thousand years, and call up a real humanitarianism out of the depths of humanity.

G. K.'s Weekly, January 2nd, 1936

*　　*　　*

THE THREE GIFTS

There were three things prefigured and promised by the gifts in the cave of Bethlehem concerning the Child who received them; that He should be crowned like a King: that He should be worshipped like a God; and that He should die like a man. And these things would sound like Eastern flattery, were it not for the third.

G. K.'s Weekly, December 12th, 1931

*　　*　　*

THE SPRING IN THE SOUL

Easter which opens on earth the gateway of the Spring, has been for all our race and culture the season of Resurrection. But in diseased conditions like our own there has come to be a standing quarrel between two schools about the order of the two ideas. Christians and all inhabiters of the ancient culture feel that Spring is the symbol of Easter. Materialists, notably all sorts of atheist anthropologists, hold that Easter was only a symbol of spring. Professors of folklore insisted that primitive men (with whom they seemed to be on very intimate terms) had made up a rather unnatural masquerade of myth, merely to cover the natural facts of experience. By the time that common sense began to pluck up courage to question what were called the Conclusions of Science, it became apparent that there were a good many questions which science could not answer, and a good many points on which her conclusions were anything but conclusive. Why should anyone want to cover up ordinary facts with an extraordinary story? Why should anybody think he could keep the grass a secret by the invention of a grass-god? And why could not primitive man be primitive enough to leave plain facts as they were? Was it not much more natural to imagine flowers or foliage as ornaments for a god or hero than to imagine a hollow idol invented only to stand between men and flowers? Is it not more sane to say that the visible renewal of the earth gives hints or signs to those who already believe in heaven? But whatever mysteries were accepted by the ancient pagans have become mere mystifications in the minds of the modern Pantheists. I imagine no man's mind was ever in so complete a muddle as the mind of the great poet Shelley when he wrote the famous line, 'If winter comes, can spring be far behind?'

To begin with, the more chilly are in the habit of reminding the poet that when Winter comes, Spring is at least a quarter of the year behind. But it will also strike the natural man (as distinct from that most unnatural man whom we call the nature-worshipper) that it would be just as easy to turn the phrase from optimism to pessimism by taking another section of the year. It would be quite as sensible to say, 'If summer comes, can autumn be far behind?' And it is probably within the range of the intelligence, even of a pantheist surveying the whole universe, to foresee that Winter will not only come, but will certainly come again. There is nothing but nonsense, therefore, in all pretences that the mere round of Nature itself is the source of our highest hopes or could by itself have evolved all that is meant by Resurrection. It is the soul that has received an unspeakable secret from heaven which it can only express in images of the earth, and naturally expresses in terms of the temporary resurrections of the earth. In other words, it uses Spring as a symbol of Easter; not Easter as a symbol of Spring. Anyone who will compare the beautiful lines of Shelley with some equally beautiful lines in one of Mr Belloc's sonnets will measure the difference made by a philosophy that happens to make sense.

> For as you pass, the natural life of things
> Proclaims the Resurrection; as you pass,
> Remembered summer shines along the grass
> And something in me of the immortal sings.

Here the poet does not talk as if next spring would last for ever; on the contrary, he talks of last summer that is already dead. But he can sing over both because of something in him different which does not die.

In this Spring more than all the other Springs, in this Easter more than all other Easters, we have to face the awful exaltation of that truth. I mean the truth that Resurrection is of faith and not of any false analogy from the senses or the seasons. Three things at least, peculiar to the present time, prevent us from identifying that hope with a revival or riot of vegetation. First, the beautiful condition to which a few centuries of progress have reduced half the landscapes of the land. Remembered summer does not shine along the grass in Pudsey or Wigan, because there is no grass to shine. The natural life of things does not proclaim the Resurrection in Sheffield and Huddersfield, because the life of things is not natural. It is only the supernatural life that dares to proclaim it there. Poets cannot describe the town landscapes as changing with the spring. They cannot say that in the spring a brighter scarlet glows in the suburban pillar-box, or in the spring the wanton policeman gets himself another crest or even another helmet. It is only human hopefulness that can see any hope in the human institution of the pillar-box; and only by a great act of faith do we affirm that policemen shall rise again from the dead. Nature cannot help us now, even as a symbol; for industrialism has destroyed the natural, but it cannot destroy the supernatural.

Second, we shall not fall into the pantheist fallacy of Shelley because it is only too likely that Nature, in the sense of immediate material resourses, will take on a sterner aspect in later and darker days; the days in which nature-worshippers become devil-worshippers. Merely natural optimists will become very unnatural pessimists – and it will be quite natural.

Lastly, the very task before us is enough to prove that things begin in the mind and that the spirit must blow its trumpet before any resurrection. For we are trying to bring back a Spring that as yet only exists in the spirit; to create grass and green things which must exist in a dream before they can exist in a landscape; the growth of which will be a miracle in the sense of something turning back the whole trend and movement of the earth. A Revolution is a mild thing compared with a Resurrection; and nothing less can raise us from the dead.

G. K.'s Weekly, March 26th, 1932

*　　　*　　　*

THE PERSON OF JESUS CHRIST

Chesterton had been invited to reply to an article in The Hibbert Journal, *which had challenged our Lord's divinity and attributed human fallibility and error to His teaching. He begins by saying that he intends to speak of 'the actual Jesus as He appears in the New Testament; not as He appears to a believer, but as He appears to anybody; as He appeared to me when I was an agnostic; as He appeared and still appears to pagans when they first read about Him.' If, therefore, he says, 'I speak of Him in this article with something that even sounds like levity, let it be understood that I am speaking for the sake of argument of a hypothetical human Jesus in the Syrian documents and not of that divine personality in whom I believe.'*

'Now, the thing that strikes me most about [the critic] is that he is wrong on the facts. He is especially wrong on the primary fact of what sort of person the Jesus of the Gospels appears to be. The whole of [his] contention is ultimately this; that when we look, so to speak, through the four windows of the Evangelists at this mysterious figure, we can see there a recognizable Jew of the first century, with the traceable limitations of such a man. Now this is exactly what we do not see. If we must put the thing profanely and without sympathy, what we see is this: an extraordinary being who would certainly have seemed as mad in one century as another, who makes a vague and vast claim to divinity, who constantly contradicts himself, who imposes impossible commands, who where he seems wrong to us would certainly have seemed quite as wrong to anybody else, who where he seems right to us is often in tune with matters not ancient but modern, such, for instance, as the adoration of children. For some of his utterances men might fairly call him a maniac; for others, men long centuries afterwards might justly call him a prophet. But what nobody can possibly call him is a Galilean of the time of Tiberius. That was not how he appeared to his own family who tried to lock him up as a lunatic. That is not how he appeared to his own nation, who lynched him, still shuddering at his earth-shaking blasphemies. The impression produced on sceptics, ancient and modern, is not that of limits, but rather of a dangerous absence of limits; a certain shapelessness and mystery of which one cannot say how far it will go. . . . The thing to say about Jesus, if you do not like Him, is that He was a megalomaniac like Nero or a mystagogue like Cagliostro. But whether or no He was small, it is plain that the Gospels are too small for Him. Whether or no He is large, He is too large for the stage. . . .

If I take it for granted (as most modern people do) that Jesus of Nazareth was one of the ordinary teachers of men, then I find Him splendid and suggestive indeed, but full of riddles and outrageous demands, by no means so workable and everyday an adviser as many heathens and many Jesuits. But if I put myself hypothetically into the other attitude, the case becomes curiously arresting and even thrilling. If I say 'Suppose the Divine did really walk and talk upon the earth, what should we be likely to think of it?' – then the foundations of my mind are moved. So far as I can form any conjecture, I think we should see in such a being exactly the perplexities that we see in the central figure of the Gospels: I think he would seem to us extreme and violent; because he would see some further development in virtue which would be for us untried. I think he would seem to us to contradict himself; because, looking down on life like a map, he would see a connection between things which to us are disconnected. I think, however, that he would always ring true to our own sense of right, but ring (so to speak) too loud and too clear. He would be too good but never too bad for us: 'Be ye perfect.' I think there would be, in the nature of things, some tragic collision between him and the humanity he had created, culminating in something that would be at once a crime and an expiation. I think he would be blamed as a hard prophet for dragging down the haughty, and blamed also as a weak sentimentalist for loving the things that cling in corners, children or beggars. I think, in short, that he would give us a sensation that he was turning all our standards upside down, and yet also a sensation that he had undeniably put them the right way up. So, if I had been a Greek sage or an Arab poet before Christ, I should have figured to myself, in a dream, what would actually happen if this earth bore secretly the father of gods and men. In the abstract, it may be that it is still only a dream. Between those who think it is a dream and those who do not, is to be waged the great war of our future in which all these frivolities will be forgotten.

Hibbert Journal, July, 1909

*   *   *

THE DIVINE COMEDY

At the beginning and at the end of all life, learned and ignorant, there is the abiding truth that in the inmost theatre of the soul of man, with a scenery of bottomless infinities and appalling abstractions, there is always going forward one ancient mystery play in which there are only two characters.

The Speaker, February 9th, 1901

*   *   *

The Dragon

The following is the last sentence of Chesterton's first published essay; it appeared in the first number of The Debater, *the journal of the famous J.D.C. at St Paul's School. In spite of its schoolboy rhetoric, it expresses something of which Chesterton's whole literary career was, in a very real sense, a fulfilment.*

Reader, when you or I meet him [the dragon], under whatever disguise, and perhaps rescue a few captives from his black cavern, may we bear a brave lance and a spotless shield through the crashing mêlée of life's narrow lists and may our wearied swords have struck fiercely on the painted crests of Imposture and Injustice when the Dark Herald comes to lead us to the pavilion of the King.

The Debater, March–April, 1891

DATE DUE

MAY 16 79			

GAYLORD PRINTED IN U.S.A.